Men-at-Arms • 467

North American Indian Tribes of the Great Lakes

Michael G. Johnson • Illustrated by Jonathan Smith

Series editor Martin Windrow

OSPREY PUBLISHING
Bloomsbury Publishing Plc

Kemp House, Chawley Park, Cumnor Hill, Oxford OX2 9PH, UK
29 Earlsfort Terrace, Dublin 2, Ireland
1385 Broadway, 5th Floor, New York, NY 10018, USA
Email: info@ospreypublishing.com
www.ospreypublishing.com

OSPREY is a trademark of Osprey Publishing Ltd

First published in Great Britain in 2011

© Osprey Publishing Ltd, 2011

Transferred to digital print on demand in 2014

A CIP catalogue record for this book is available from the British Library.

Print ISBN: 978 1 84908 459 8
ePub: 978 1 78096 499 7
ePDF: 978 1 84908 460 4

Editorial by Martin Windrow
Page layouts by Melissa Orrom Swan, Oxford
Index by Sandra Shotter
Originated by United Graphics Pte
Typeset in Helvetica Neue and ITC New Baskerville
Printed and bound in Great Britain

The Woodland Trust
Osprey Publishing is supporting the Woodland Trust, the UK's leading woodland conservation charity, by funding the dedication of trees.

www.ospreypublishing.com
To find out more about our authors and books visit our website. Here you will find extracts, author interviews, details of forthcoming events and the option to sign-up for our newsletter.

Dedication
This book is dedicated to the life and work of the English artist and illustrator Richard Hook (1938–2010), with whom the author had a long and happy association.

Acknowledgements
The author wishes to express his thanks to the following, who gave their time during the preparation of the text: Tim O'Sullivan and Polly Fitzwalter, in Britain; and Neil and Jana Oppendike, of Illinios, who made it possible for the author to visit some of the sites mentioned in the text. For help in securing images, thanks also go to: Deborah Holder, Archives of Ontario; Gary Hood, West Point Museum, NY; John Hart, New York State Historical Association; Susan Otto, Milwaukee Public Museum; and Marcia Anderson, Minnesota Historical Society.

Artist's note
Readers may care to note that the original paintings from which the color plates in this book were prepared are available for private sale. All reproduction copyright whatsoever is retained by the Publishers. All enquiries should be addressed to:

Jonathan Smith
107 Ryeworth Road
Charlton Kings
Gloucestershire
GL52 6LS
UK

Email: jonathanpsmith59@yahoo.co.uk

The Publishers regret that they can enter into no correspondance upon this matter.

TITLE PAGE **Winnebago (Ho-Chunk) men, c.1900, photographed near Black River Falls or Tomah, WI. Several wear buckskin leggings, beaded sashes and armbands. The man at left holds a bow and arrows; second left has a cloth apron beaded in typical Winnebago abstract floral designs; third left holds an eagle-feather fan; and fourth left, standing, holds a "gunstock" warclub. Their faces show differing degrees of mixed ancestry.**

NORTH AMERICAN INDIAN TRIBES OF THE GREAT LAKES

THE GREAT LAKES REGION

The Great Lakes Region was dominated by water and forest. The thousands of interconnected lakes and rivers afforded the Indians the means to travel long distances by canoe, with short land journeys between by "*portage*" (the French term for carrying canoes from water to water). While the five Great Lakes drain the huge water system from the north and west, south of them tributaries drain into the two major river valleys of the Mississippi and Ohio.

Natural vegetation varies throughout the area. In the north, on the now-Canadian side, coniferous forests of spruce, fir, jack pine, tamarack and cedar gradually give way southward to mixed coniferous and deciduous woodland, adding maple, beech, birch, hemlock, and finally basswood, oak, hickory, cottonwood, willow and elm, with deciduous species predominating in the Ohio valley. Before European contact small tracts were no doubt cleared by burning, particularly on the Prairie-Woodland borders where indigenous peoples practiced agriculture. From the early 17th century the ecology was increasingly disturbed by the arrival of Europeans, with the selective trapping of fur-bearing animals, and from the 18th century there was major and increasing forest clearance and drainage of land for lumber and European agriculture. The river and lake travel systems were also used by European explorers, missionaries and fur-traders, and by the early years of the 18th century the French had already linked their Canadian and Gulf of Mexico colonies by regular routes.

In the Great Lakes region four major subsistence patterns are identified: domesticated plants, hunting, fishing, and gathering wild rice. Domesticated Indian corn (maize), beans, and squashes were the basic foods of the tribes of the Ohio valley, lower Ontario (the Huron), New York (the Iroquois), southern Wisconsin and southern Michigan. Nevertheless, all the agricultural Indians also hunted, fished and collected wild plant foods. The major subsistence pattern was hunting. In the north, Indians were completely dependent upon moose, caribou, bear, beaver and fish. In the south, various deer, elk, buffalo (bison), bear, turkey and other species were important sources of food,

Photographed c.1900, this mature man is probably an Ojibwa (Chippewa). His headdress is a braided woollen turban with eagle feathers and V-cut ribbons. His multiple bead necklace is of Plains style; his woollen leggings are bound with woven beaded garters with fringed ties.

3

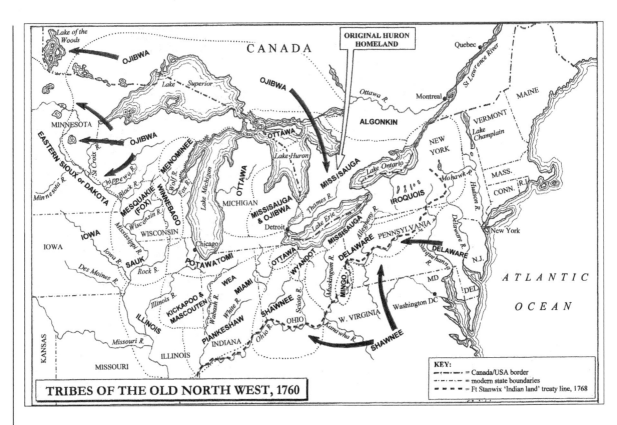

TRIBES OF THE OLD NORTH WEST, 1760

KEY:
−·−·−·− = Canada/USA border
−·−·−·− = modern state boundaries
− − − − = Ft Stanwix 'Indian land' treaty line, 1768

along with the storage of corn. The Ojibwa, Ottawa and some Iroquoian groups living around the periphery of the Great Lakes developed a food economy centered on fishing, with occasional gardening and maple sugar production. Finally, west and southwest of lakes Michigan and Superior wild rice provided a major food source for the Menominee, some Winnebago and Dakota (Eastern Sioux), although hunting, and for some the cultivation of corn, were also important.

Archaeologists have identified three broad cultural traditions among the late prehistoric Northeastern Indians, which manifest themselves in ceramic remains from at least AD 1000. These are the Woodland culture of the Atlantic coastal area and upper Midwest; the Upper Mississippian culture of the upper Ohio and upper Mississippi river valleys; and the Mississippian culture of southern Illinois and Indiana. In general terms the Woodland tradition divides into two subgroups, which approximate to the Algonquian- and Iroquois-speaking peoples. The Upper Mississippian culture also separates into those of Algonquian and those of Siouan background, including the probable ancestors of the historic Shawnee. The Mississippian cultural tradition which predominated in the Gulf and lower Mississippi valley is marginal to Great Lakes prehistory, but some influential centers did exist in the southern Midwest and southern Wisconsin.

In the early historic period, c.1600, the Indian population in the region of the upper, western three Great Lakes – Superior, Michigan and Huron – was about 130,000. Perhaps 60,000 were Huron and their related Iroquoian tribes of Ontario; the other, mostly Algonquian-speaking tribes included the closely related Ojibwa, Potawatomi and Ottawa. (The Winnebago, however, are Siouan in speech.) The Hurons

ABOVE RIGHT In 1673 the French reached the Mississippi via the Fox and Wisconsin rivers. By the mid-1700s French fur posts lined the Mississipi valley down to Louisiana, and extended out onto the Parklands and Prairies. However, control of the upper Mississippi was delayed during 1712–38 by war with the Mesquakie (Fox), who struggled unsuccessfully to unite the tribes of the region to oppose French passage across Wisconsin and trade with the Sioux.

After Britain acquired French Canada in 1760, many French fur traders – both licensed (voyageurs) and illegal (coureurs du bois) – remained active, scattered throughout the Great Lakes and upper Mississippi regions, but the management and major profits of the trade were taken over by English, Scottish and New England merchants. Pelts and trade goods flowed through the main centers at Michilimackinac (from 1781, Mackinac), Grand Portage and Detroit, while Prairie du

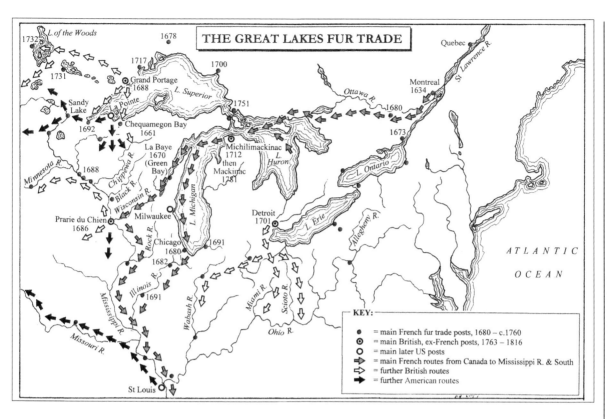

THE GREAT LAKES FUR TRADE

KEY:
● = main French fur trade posts, 1680 – c.1760
◉ = main British, ex-French posts, 1763 – 1816
○ = main later US posts
⇨ = main French routes from Canada to Mississippi R. & South
⇨ = further British routes
➡ = further American routes

Chien was established to trade with western tribes such as the Sioux.

The United States purchased the Louisiana Territory in 1803, and with it St Louis, key to the Missouri River and Rocky Mountains. After the War of 1812 with Britain the USA established control of the Northwest, and St Louis became the leading center for the fur trade – though this declined steadily, and traders shifted their investments to land, lumber and mining as settlers poured westward.
(Maps by John Richards)

were extensive farmers, the Ojibwa primarily hunters, and Menominee subsistence was based upon wild rice to a greater degree than other groups. The Ottawa and Potawatomi tended to hunt in small family groups, while the Sauk, Mesquakie (Fox) and southern tribes undertook communal hunts on the prairies; the Winnebago and Menominee seem to have been intermediate between these patterns.

European contact

The arrival of European explorers, missionaries and fur-traders brought changes in native technology, with the introduction of metal weapons, tools and utensils, blankets and other trade cloth, porcelain and glass beads, to replace native buckskin clothing decorated with shell and bone beads and dyed porcupine quills. But trade goods never completely eliminated native technology, and such Indian items as moccasins, snowshoes and canoes were adopted in their turn by Europeans. By c.1750 firearms had largely replaced the bow and arrow and, importantly, colonial wars and the fur trade had also rearranged tribal locations.

From their bases in Montreal and Quebec the French were quick to make use of Indian trails and canoe routes. By the end of the 17th century they had a route from New France to the Mississippi, via the Ottawa and French rivers to lakes Huron and Michigan, then via Green Bay, the Fox and Wisconsin rivers to the Mississippi, with few portages on the way. This opened up the whole core area of the Great Lakes to French missionaries and traders, and, in the early 18th century, opened the Illinois region to permanent French settlements.

By contrast, the British colonies along the Atlantic seaboard faced a natural barrier to westward exploration on the same scale as their

Early 1820s: Ojibwa family in birchbark canoe arriving near Red River, Manitoba, after traveling from their homelands around Lake Superior to trade for British goods. Note the distinctive prow and stern shape of the Ojibwa canoe. (Detail from painting by Peter Rindisbacher; West Point Museum Art Collection, US Military Academy, West Point, NY)

French competitors: the Appalachian chain, and in particular the Allegheny Mountains, barred the way to the "Ohio country." This area – also sometimes referred to as the "Old Northwest" – was largely the present-day states of Ohio and Indiana. During the 17th century, Iroquois war parties criss-crossed this area in an attempt to hijack the burgeoning fur trade between the French and the Algonquian nations who, consequently, seem largely to have vacated the region for parts of Wisconsin and Michigan. Iroquois war parties reached the Illinois Indians and the Mississippi River, and perhaps even beyond. It was not until after the "Great Peace" brokered by the French at Montreal in 1701 that these Iroquois forays decreased, and the historic tribes of the Ohio region returned to settle there once more.

The Ohio country also became home for disaffected Delawares and Munsees from New York and New Jersey, and Mohicans from New England, who had suffered the devastating effects of the first waves of European settlement further east. The Miami relinquished their eastern territory to the predatory Shawnee from the Cumberland River region to the south, and to re-grouped Huron (now called Wyandot) and Ottawa from the north. A number of tribes vaguely reported in the 17th century were perhaps integrated into Iroquois groups who lived permanently in the area, such as the Mingoes, or the 19th-century Seneca of Sandusky. The Iroquois league continued to exert control over the affairs of some tribes and villages during the 18th century by appointing "half-kings" – a sort of ambassadors – to the Ohio Indians.

In the west, the Sioux were at one time actively engaged in the collection of wild rice in parts of northern Wisconsin and Minnesota, which brought them into conflict with those Ojibwa who were moving west in promotion of the fur trade. The Ojibwa, who already possessed firearms, expelled the Sioux totally from the Wisconsin area, and eventually from the northern two-thirds of Minnesota, including their traditional homeland around Mille Lacs. After the Sioux war of 1862 only four small Eastern Sioux communities remained in southern Minnesota.[1]

The principal peoples of the region around the three upper Great Lakes were as follows.

PRINCIPAL INDIAN NATIONS

Huron, Tionontati (Petun), and Wyandot (Wendat)

The Huron, and their close relatives the Tionontati or Tobacco Nation, inhabited present-day Ontario on the peninsula formed by lakes Huron and Erie. The name Huron apparently derives from the French description of the warriors' hairstyles (French priests visited them from

---

[1] For further details of Iroquois, Delaware and Sioux history, see Men-at-Arms Nos. 395, *Tribes of the Iroquois Confederacy*; 428, *Indian Tribes of the New England Frontier*; & 344, *Tribes of the Sioux Nation*.

1615, and permanent Jesuit missions began in 1626). They probably had a combined population of 60,000 at the beginning of the 17th century; however, within not much more than 50 years their numbers had been reduced drastically by disease, famine, and war, and the remaining people had been driven from their homeland.

The Huron were an Iroquoian-speaking nation related to the Iroquois of New York, the Neutral of southern Ontario, the Wenro on the Niagara River, and the Erie (Raccoon Nation) on the southern shore of Lake Erie. Many Huron villages were protected by palisades up to 30ft high, made of poles in three rows, with galleries and watchtowers. Inside were rows of longhouses of elm, ash and cedar bark up to 150ft long, 30ft wide and 20ft high, with sleeping platforms on either side of central passages. Each longhouse could be home for up to 24 related women of the same clan; it was divided into family compartments with woven mats, and accommodated cooking utensils and a supply of corn and firewood for winter. The Hurons and Tionontati obtained most of their food by farming, but also gathered wild foods, hunted and fished. Village sites were usually moved about every 10 years, when cropland and local sources of firewood were exhausted. There were three Huron clans, tracing descent through the female line, and – as in most tribes – intermarriage within a clan was forbidden. When French Jesuits reported their culture in their early 17th-century annual "Relations," there were four subtribes of the Huron: the Rock, Cord, Bear and Deer each had their own chief and council. At the death of a clan chief his name and position passed to his sister's son, a male of his own clan.

Because of the Hurons' advantageous position with the French as middlemen in the beaver-fur trade, the Iroquois first invaded Huron country in 1648 and sacked St Joseph, and in March 1649 they destroyed St Ignace and St Louis, thus breaking the Hurons' monopoly. Hundreds were carried into captivity, and others fled north or west; those remaining were completely demoralized, turning against and killing the French priests whom they blamed for their misfortunes. In turn the Tionontati, Erie and Neutral nations all suffered the same fate. A few Hurons escaped to the French settlements near Quebec, where a number of their descendants have survived until the present day. Other Huron and Tionontati fugitives sought refuge on Christian Island in Georgian Bay, and it is from these survivors that the Wyandot of later history descended. From here they moved west to Michilimackinac, then to Manitoulin Island, Green Bay, Chequamegon Bay (along with some Ottawas) during the 1660s, and even to Illinois tribal country on the Mississippi. By 1670 they returned to Michilimackinac, and later to the Detroit area, to sites near Sandwich, Ontario, and by 1745 to the Sandusky River in Ohio.

Under the leadership of Orontory or Nicholas ("War Pole," q.v.), in 1748 the Wyandot conspired with warriors from other tribes to destroy the French posts at Detroit and elsewhere, but his plot was revealed to the French, his confederacy collapsed, and his villages along the Sandusky River were destroyed. Nevertheless, Wyandots became an important element in the new multi-tribal groups now in the Ohio country alongside Delaware and

About 190 years after Rindisbacher made his painting, the author photographed the stern of this Ojibwa canoe at Waswagoning Indian Village, Lac du Flambeau, Wisconsin. Note too the birchbark torch on a pole, used for night fishing, and the three-point fishing spear.

Mary Kelley, a Wyandot woman photographed in c.1911. The Wyandot were descended from the Huron; once the largest tribe in the western Great Lakes region and the most important ally of the French, they were drastically weakened and driven from their lands by Iroquois invasions as early as the middle decades of the 17th century.

Shingwaukonce, "Little Pine" (1773–1854), Ojibwa chief of the Garden River band at the eastern end of Lake Superior on the Canadian shore. After fighting with the British in the War of 1812, he repaired relations with the Americans. He was succeeded by his son George Shingwauk (1839–1920), who successfully promoted harmony between traditionalists and Christian converts, many of whom had been forcibly removed from Sault Ste Marie. (Drawing by Martin Somerville, Montreal, c.1840)

Shawnee, and they supported the British in the War of 1812. They gradually sold their lands around Detroit and Sandusky, and in 1842 the tribe, now largely acculturated, moved to Kansas. In 1867 the majority moved again, to Indian Territory (now Oklahoma), where a reservation was provided in the northeastern corner of the future state. A small Wyandot band survived near present-day Amhurstburg, Ontario, until 1896, becoming enfranchised; they have descendants in Trenton near Detroit. In 2000, 1,850 mixed Wyandot descendants were reported. Those whose ancestors fled to Quebec in 1649 are still counted at the village of Lorette, and 3,012 "Wendat" were reported in 2005. Their language is extinct.

Ojibwa (Chippewa, or Anishinabe)

The Ojibwa first encountered by French travelers were living on abundant year-round fishing in the area where lakes Superior and Huron adjoin at Sault Ste Marie; the French called them Saulteurs. The total population of the Ojibwa, Ottawa and Potawatomi of the central Great Lakes may originally have been around 50,000 at the time of first contact, of which at least 35,000 were probably Ojibwa, the remainder being split about equally between the other two tribes. The popular names Ojibwa or Ojibwe, and in the US Chippewa, apparently derive from "to roast till puckered up," referring to the puckered seam on their moccasins. The earliest known Ojibwa bands at the Sault were the Amikwa (Beaver), Nokwet (Bear), and Marameg (Catfish).

Ojibwa living north of Lake Superior were divided into bands each of about 500 people, living by hunting alone over an area of at least 1,200 square miles. To survive the harsh winters, the bands divided into smaller hunting units. Moose, caribou, bear, beaver and many other animals were hunted with bow and arrows and spears, or trapped. In summer family units gathered at good fishing places, where whitefish and sturgeon were taken in huge quantities. During the 17th century the Ojibwa seem to have begun an expansion to the south shore of Lake Superior, where some corn was raised, but this was less important than hunting and fishing; by the 1730s some bands were gathering the wild rice that grew in abundance around many lakes and marshes. An important spring activity for some bands was the collection of maple sap for making maple sugar.

By about 1692 the Ojibwa had replaced the refugee Huron and Ottawa as the principal Indian people at Chequamegon Bay on the south shore of Lake Superior, which became an important center for the fur trade, and also for the reformation of their religious rituals; they adapted to the new conditions brought by white contact, while remaining in continued isolation in the general Great Lakes area. Because of their largely hunting and trapping traditions the Ojibwa perhaps fitted more comfortably into the changes brought by the fur trade, since they occupied lands least suitable for farming, and remote from the increasing pressure of white settlement. Their continued southern drift from Lake Superior was probably hastened by white traders' demand for beaver, which were disappearing from the northern and eastern Ojibwa domains. The establishment of villages in the Lac du

Flambeau, Lac Court Oreilles and Fond du Lac areas of present-day Wisconsin and Minnesota brought the Ojibwa into contact with the Eastern Sioux (Dakota); they defeated the Dakota at Flambeau Lake and later at Mole Lake in 1745, forcing the Sioux beyond the Mississippi River and ultimately into southern Minnesota. During the 18th century they also compelled the Fox (Mesquakie) to leave northern Wisconsin, making the interior safe for their own villages and hunting camps.

By the end of the 18th century the Ojibwa had reached the Wisconsin, Chippewa and St Croix rivers, and as far southwest as Mille Lacs. By this time European firearms, metal spear- and arrowheads, tools and utensils, traps and fish hooks had made subsistence much easier – but the fur-traders also brought alcohol and European diseases, which had devastating effects. While many Ojibwa moved south and west, another body of their people overran the Ontario peninsula between lakes Huron and Erie – land long claimed by the Iroquois by right of conquest; these Ojibwa bands are usually referred to as Mississauga.

The social and political organizations of the Ojibwa were much less elaborate than those of the Huron, although there were clan and band chiefs. There was no Ojibwa "tribe" as such, since this people were scattered over a huge area. In time the Ojibwa settled through much of the northern two-thirds of Minnesota, at Red Lake, Leech Lake, along the Rainy River and Lake of the Woods, and into the Parklands of North Dakota, Manitoba and Saskatchewan, with one band even reaching British Columbia. However, there was a tribal unity of sorts, based upon language, kinship, and clan membership, which allowed individual families to move great distances to join relatives. The kinship system and social organization was based on patrilineal clans similar to those of the Ottawa and Potawatomi (who by native accounts were all descended from the same people). The clans carried animal totemic titles – the Crane, Loon, Hawk, Gull, Pike, Otter, Moose, Caribou, Wolf, Lynx, and so forth. Later, during the fur-trade period, the mixed-blood clans of part-British descent adopted the Lion as their symbol, and those of American descent the Eagle.

Some bands and warriors took part with other tribes in all the wars along the old Northwest frontier, including the Pontiac Rebellion of 1763 and the War of 1812. Over the years that followed they made several land cessions in Michigan (1819–36), Wisconsin (1826–42) and Minnesota (1847–63) to the US, and in Canada to the British Crown between 1850 and 1929. One small band of Swan Creek and Black River Ojibwa from southern Michigan left the Great Lakes area to join a small group of Munsee Delawares in Kansas, but most bands remained on fractions of their old lands. Over the years they have intermarried freely, at first with French and then with British and Americans, leaving few families entirely free of European blood.

During the 19th century and after the establishment of the reservations their traditional lifestyle, largely based on seasonal movements for subsistence, faded rapidly. More than 400 Wisconsin Ojibwa died while attempting to collect their annuities from far-off Sandy Lake, Minnesota. After 1887 some reservations were "allotted" – i.e. communal lands were broken up; their economy moved to logging, and ultimately to tourism and off-reservation employment. In 2000 the US census reported 105,907 "Chippewa" in the United States;

Ju-ah-kis-gaw, an Ojibwa woman painted by George Catlin, c.1834. She wears a black strap-dress with red shoulder straps and multi-colored separate sleeves; note the head-bow of the cradleboard, and its multi-colored beaded cloth wrapping. Her face is painted red down to the bottom of the nose.

in 2005, 91,685 were listed in Canada as Ojibwa, with many more listed as mixed with Cree or regarded as Métis (mixed-bloods). They are therefore one of the largest tribes of North America, and are famous for their canoe-building, birch-bark utensils, and the floral-pattern beadwork that adorned their ceremonial regalia. Culturally, the Ojibwa have maintained until recent times elements of traditional culture, such as the Medicine Lodge and Drum or Dream Dance (see under "Beliefs and Rituals," and Plate E), and Pan-Indian events are held on most present-day reservations.

ABOVE: **Ojibwa family traveling in summertime, Red River, Manitoba, early 1820s; by this date bands of Ojibwa were living permanently on the borders of the Parklands and Prairies.The woman wears a strap-dress of blue trade-cloth, and beaded red sleeves and leggings; the warrior wears a natural-color blanket, and carries a bow, musket and tomahawk. Note that one of the dogs pulls a Plains-style travois, while others are loaded with bundles and mats. (Detail from painting by Peter Rindisbacher; West Point Museum Art Collection, US Military Academy, West Point, NY)**

Ottawa (Odawa) and Potawatomi

These tribes were culturally similar. The Ottawa (Odawa) name comes from a generic northern Algonquian verb, "to trade," and was applied to four large autonomous groups who signed the peace treaty at Montreal in 1701; before then they had often lived with the Hurons in various locations around the Great Lakes. The name Potawatomi derives from "people of the place of the fire." The Ottawa were located principally in what is now northeastern Michigan and on islands in Lake Huron, while the Potawatomi lived in western Michigan, although by 1634 at least some Potawatomi were living on the southern shore of Lake Michigan, and by 1700 along the Wisconsin shore and in the vicinity of Chicago in northern Illinois. After 1650 the Ottawa began to move westward to escape the Iroquois, who were extending their fur-gathering domain at the expense of their neighbors. At least one band of Ottawa and Huron refugees occupied a village in the Chequamegon Bay area, while others lived around Green Bay, and later on the upper peninsula of Michigan and parts of the lower peninsula; in their later history this group became particularly associated with Manitoulin Island on the Canadian shore of Lake Huron, where they mixed with Ojibwa and Potawatomi. Others moved as far south and east as Ohio, and Beaver Creek, Pennsylvania.

The Ottawa and Potawatomi were semi-sedentary; in summer they lived in villages and practiced agriculture, separating into family groups in the fall and departing for their winter hunting grounds, where they remained until spring. Hunting and fishing were male occupations, while women planted crops, gathered the harvest, and collected wild nuts, berries and rice. Both men and women collected maple sap and converted it into sugar. Their villages consisted mainly of dome-shaped wigwams of saplings covered with cattail mats and bark, or larger bark-covered lodges; some villages, usually located along a river or lake with access via canoes, were protected by circular log palisades.

The Ottawa and Potawatomi were subdivided into a number of bands that possessed their own territories and were politically independent, though with connections through family, clan and kinship ties. A clan was a group who traced their blood ancestors to a single male, and

BELOW: **Mah-we-do-ke-shiek, "Spirit of the Skies," an Ojibwa chief photographed in the 1860s; apparently he was noted for his courage. His *capote* appears to be made from a Hudson's Bay blanket. (Photo Whitney & Zimmerman)**

marriage to a member of the same clan was forbidden. Ottawa clan titles included the Sturgeon, Turtle, Swan, Crane, Owl, Bear, Elk, Moose, Otter, Thunder, and Moon, and those of Potawatomi clans were very similar. A band of *c.*400 people would comprise a dozen or so extended families; ties of kinship recognized all fathers' brothers as "father" and mothers' sisters as "mother," extending the terms to in-laws of the same generation.

During the 1820s–30s the Ottawa ceded most of their territory to the US, moving first to Kansas and then to Indian Territory. The remainder lived throughout Michigan and Ontario, the largest number on Manitoulin Island. The Ottawa numbered 6,432 in the US census of 2000, but in Canada they are not returned separately from the Ojibwa.

The Potawatomi actively sided with the French until the end of the French and Indian War; they were also prominent in the Pontiac War of 1763-64, and took up arms against the United States during the Revolution and the War of 1812. After the peace of 1815 they sold their lands piecemeal in two separate bodies – the Potawatomi of the Woods, and of the Prairies – uniting in Kansas in 1846, with some re-formed as the Citizen band moving to Oklahoma in 1868. Others moved to Ontario and mixed with Ojibwa and Ottawa; four other groups survived in Michigan, and one mainly in Forest County in northern Wisconsin. The 2000 census reported 15,817 Potawatomi in the US, and in 2005 a Canadian fraction was numbered at 290. All present-day descendants of Great Lakes Indians, and particularly those whose forebears were forced to live in Oklahoma, are now of largely mixed ancestry. Although some participate in Pan-Indian events, their traditional culture, native language and customs have largely disappeared. By 2000 only 50 speakers of the Potawatomi tongue remained in the US, but there are several hundred Ottawa-speakers in Canada.

Menominee (Menomini)

The name is derived from the Ojibwa term meaning "wild rice men," and they probably numbered about 3,000 people when first known to whites. They originally lived along the Menominee River, with their main village at the mouth of this river on Green Bay. They spoke a dialect of Algonquian closer to Sauk and Fox than to Ojibwa, but their closest cultural relations – in kinship systems, social and political organization, and religious beliefs – were with their Winnebago neighbors to the south. Their subsistence depended on hunting, fishing and gathering, but the harvesting of the wild rice that grew abundantly in their territory was also a major activity. Their cultivation of corn was limited, but they collected wild plant foods.

The Menominee lived in sedentary villages, in lodges of bark and woven mats similar to those of the Winnebago and other tribes to the south. They were excellent weavers of mats and bags of twined vegetable fiber and sometimes spun buffalo hair; these bags were decorated with designs of humans, animals, and mythological birds and underwater creatures. With the arrival of European trade goods they became skilled in beadwork, ribbonwork, and the use of the cloth that largely replaced skin and fur for clothing by the 18th century.

The recorded history of the tribe began in 1634 when the French explorer Jean Nicollet passed through their country, and in 1668 a

Simon Kaquados, Wisconsin Potawatomi, c.1915. He succeeded Chief Charles Kishek as leader of the Potawatomi of Forest County and Arpin, and in the early 20th century became their principal historian.

Ke-wah-ten, "The North Wind," a Menominee woman painted by Paul Kane in 1846. She wears multiple silver earrings all round the rims of her ears, and silver brooches.

Louise Amor, a Menominee woman photographed in c.1915, with a blanket and skirt richly decorated with appliqué ribbonwork. The southern Great Lakes tribes excelled at this craft, and no doubt took it to the Missouri River tribes and to Oklahoma after some tribes were forced to relocate westward in the 19th century. See also Plate G4.

French fur-trader named Perrot was recorded as transporting a cargo of pelts from La Baye (Green Bay) to New France. By 1671 the French reached a formal agreement at Sault Ste Marie with 14 tribes, including the Menominee, and soon brought the whole western Great Lakes area into the French sphere of influence, and its Indians into the fur-trade economy. Jesuits were also active in Menominee territory from 1669.

Menominee warriors helped the French in their wars against the Fox during the 1730s, and later against the British – Menominees were among Langlade's Indians who destroyed Braddock's force on the Monongahela in 1755. Although there was considerable intermarriage with French trappers and settlers, when the British succeeded the French after 1760 the Menominee became their allies, fighting with them against Pontiac's coalition in 1763 and against the Americans in the Revolution. In 1794 the region became part of the United States under the provisions of the Jay Treaty, but the Menominee again sided with the British in the War of 1812.

In 1848 the Menominee ceded their lands to the US in return for a reservation in Minnesota, which did not materialize; instead, in 1852 some 2,000 people moved to Keshena on the Wolf River within their own territory, which by a treaty of 1854 became the Menominee Reservation. (However, 300 mixed-bloods had accepted payment to relinquish tribal affiliation, and were thenceforth no longer "Menominees.") The death-toll during these movements of 1852–58 was very heavy; however, the reservation was covered with good timber, which later brought the tribe some economic benefits from a century of activity in the logging industry. During the second half of the 19th century the old economy of hunting, fishing, and gathering wild rice greatly diminished, along with most visible expressions of native culture.

The tribe provided a number of men for the Union cause in the Civil War, and for the US Army in the Spanish-American War; in World War II, 400 tribal members served in the US armed services. In 1954, 3,270 had tribal membership, of whom 2,677 lived on the reservation, but only 71 were known to be full-blood. The tribe's advanced acculturation encouraged a policy of complete termination of federal supervision, and in 1961 a process was completed by which the reservation became an integrated part of the state of Wisconsin, with a per capita distribution of tribal assets. However, this was revoked in 1973. In 2001 the Bureau of Indian Affairs reported 8,074 members, although the community at Zoar has considerable Potawatomi ancestry. Only about 40 fluent speakers of the Menominee language remained in 2000.

Winnebago (Ho-Chunk)

This tribe spoke a Siouan language, which probably links them historically with the Siouan peoples of the upper Mississippi valley before they moved west; pottery finds also confirm this association. Apparently the name Winnebago comes from the Ojibwa term Winipig ("filthy water"), a reference to Green Bay, the algae-rich but malodorous body of water that was their original home. They called themselves Hochagra ("people of parent speech"). When first encountered by the

French in the 17th century they lived in northeastern Wisconsin, but in later times they moved south to Lake Winnebago, and ultimately to the middle Wisconsin River region.

Their habitat allowed the raising of corn, beans, squash, and tobacco, and they also collected wild rice, nuts and berries. After the crops were harvested they went on a communal buffalo hunt on the prairies southwest of their semi-permanent villages. They lived in dome-shaped wigwams 12ft to 40ft in length, 10–20ft wide and about 15ft high, covered with woven reed mats or bark on a frame of bent saplings, and with internal platforms. Their kinship system was similar to the Sauk and Mesquakie, and dissimilar to the Ojibwa-Ottawa system, which tended to separate generations. The Winnebago stressed lineage in the male line through a mother's brother, whose male descendants were also termed "uncles." The daughters of these uncles were called "mothers," and their children were one's "brothers and sisters." This system, ignoring differences of generation, allowed a wider spread of wealth and prestige, which also reflected the abundant food supply and sedentary lifestyle of a milder and richer natural environment than that available to the Ojibwa. Children were born into the clan of the father; marriage within the clan was not allowed, nor within the tribal division to which one belonged. There were two divisions: the Upper or Air phratry, and the Lower or Earth, each with its own animal-totem clan fraternities. The Thunderbird was the leading clan of the Upper division, and the Bear that of the Lower division, each with its own obligations for war, policing, and arranging buffalo hunts.

The Winnebago were known to whites since 1634, when Nicollet reported them living on Green Bay, but by 1671 reports place them on Lake Winnebago after a war with the Illinois Indians. In 1766 Jonathan Carver found them on the Fox River in Wisconsin. During this period they were on friendly terms with most of the surrounding tribes, and with the French until the fall of French Canada in 1760. They sided with Britain during the War of 1812, and were among the several tribes that helped defeat the Americans at the battle of the River Raisin ("Frenchtown") in January 1813; this episode was notorious for the subsequent massacre of 60 disarmed American prisoners.

Part of the tribe remained hostile to the Americans; Red Bird's warriors killed a few lead-miners in southern Wisconsin in 1827, and southern Winnebagos aided Black Hawk's Sauks during the war of 1832. Following treaties at Prairie du Chien in 1825, 1832 and 1837, the Winnebago ceded to the US most of their territory in Wisconsin for a reservation beyond the Mississippi, and in 1846 they moved to Minnesota (during a period in which they lost a quarter of their numbers to smallpox). Following the Sioux war of 1862 the white people of Minnesota demanded that they be moved again; they were forced first to the Crow Creek Reservation in South Dakota, but in 1863 they were finally located on the Omaha Reservation, Nebraska. During this period of great hardship individual

Hoowabneka, "Little Chief," a Winnebago who fought for the British in the War of 1812. He visited Washington, DC, in 1824, and signed the treaty with the US at Prairie du Chien the following year – note the "peace medal." He wears silver armlets; his face paint is red (hairline) above black, with small green details, and his body and arm paint is red on his right side, green on his left. (Lithograph from McKenney & Hall)

"Standing Buffalo," a Winnebago photographed in the 1860s. He wears a head roach; metal earrings; necklaces, armlets and wristlets; an apron, buckskin leggings with fur garters (skunk?), and moccasins. He carries an eagle-feather fan. (Photo Gurnsey & Illingworth, Sioux City, IA)

families filtered back to Wisconsin, obtaining small parcels of land scattered throughout their old homelands, particularly around Black River Falls and Tomah.

In 1910 there were reportedly 1,063 in Nebraska and 1,270 in Wisconsin. In 2001 the same groups were numbered at 4,033 and 6,145 respectively, the Wisconsin portion now being called Ho-Chunk. In common with most of the Great Lakes tribes, they became largely acculturated during the 20th century. They have been recipients of the Peyote cult (Native American Church – see under Plate E), and participants in Pan-Indian events. By 2000, fewer than 250 fluent speakers of the Winnebago language remained.

Sauk (Sac) and Fox (Mesquakie)

The Sauk and Fox have long been associated with Wisconsin's deciduous forest zone, and later the grassy prairie of northern Illinois and Iowa. However, there is evidence that the Sauks' earliest known home was the eastern peninsula of Michigan, along with the Potawatomi and Mascouten. The term Sauk, meaning "people of the inlet" or alternatively "yellow earth people," may be a reference to Saginaw Bay, a probable early location. Despite a long and close association with the Sauk, to whom they were probably related, the Fox or Mesquakie ("red earth people") seem to have lived on the Fox and Wolf rivers and around Lake Winnebago when first encountered by whites. Neither tribe probably had an original population of more than 2,000. The Sauk were first reported in the Jesuit "Relations" for 1640, when the Hurons referred to them as "westerners." In 1671 they were reported around Green Bay, having been driven out of their original habitat.

The villages of the Sauk and Fox consisted of clusters of oval-shaped wigwams, made of woven rush and cattail mats tied to arched saplings. Their subsistence was based upon a combination of farming and hunting; villages were usually occupied from April to October, with the winters spent in small temporary hunting encampments. Women planted and cultivated corn, beans, and squash in fields cleared by burning the previous year's dead cornstalks. After the harvest entire villages moved onto the prairies for the winter buffalo hunt; elk, deer, bear and beaver were also hunted in their forest regions. They made some use of dugout canoes; under the influence of the fur-traders they learned the use of bark canoes and snowshoes, but these were not typical of their traditional culture. The clothing of the Sauk and Fox was similar to that of the Winnebago and Miami.

While their political organization more closely resembled that of the Potawatomi, their kinship systems were also similar to those of the Winnebago and Miami. The Sauk and Fox stressed lineage through one's mother's brothers and their male descendants, thus extending relationships beyond each generation. They were divided into patrilineal clans whose mythical founders had supernatural powers derived from animals such as the Bear, Wolf, Fox, Elk, Swan, Partridge and Bass. Their two main religious rituals were the clan festival held twice a year, which offered thanksgiving to the spirits for a new agricultural season, and in the summer when the fields ripened; and the

Midewiwin (q.v.), an elaborately organized society entered by invitation and payment, to ensure long life and health. The Tama Mesquakie, like the Mexican Kickapoo (q.v.), retained these religious observances until recent times.

The Fox conceived a hatred of the French traders who had followed the old Indian trail from Lake Michigan to the Mississippi via the Fox and Wisconsin rivers, exploiting the fur trade of central Wisconsin, and aligning other tribes such as the Ojibwa against the Fox. They planned an attack on Fort Detroit in 1712, which failed, and the French subsequently carried out a long war of destruction against them. During the 1720s the Sauk were sympathetic toward their friends the Fox without totally joining them in all-out war against the French, but had friendly relations with the Spanish beyond the Mississippi. They were met by Jonathan Carver in 1766 on the Wisconsin River, and by Peter Pond in 1773.

In 1804 they began a series of treaties with the US, which required the Sauk to move west of the Mississippi – a directive that many refused. Warriors fought with Tecumseh in the War of 1812; and in 1832 some attempted to resettle on old Sauk territory at Rock Island and along the Rock River, Illinois. This so-called Black Hawk War (q.v.) resulted in defeat at Bad Axe Creek, Wisconsin, with the death of many women and children. In 1837 the Sauk and Fox made their last cessions in Iowa and reunited in Kansas; but internal dissensions split them, and during the 1850s the Fox purchased land for a new home at Tama, Iowa, which has remained their settlement. In 1867 the Sauk mostly moved from Kansas to a reservation in Oklahoma.

In 1820 the combined population of the two tribes was estimated at 3,000. In 1909, 352 were reported in Iowa (nearly all Fox), 536 in Oklahoma (mostly Sauk), and 87 in Kansas (also chiefly Sauk). In 2001 the Bureau of Indian Affairs numbered the same groups at 1,260 (Iowa), 3,025 (Oklahoma), and 433 (Kansas-Nebraska). The Sauk and Fox near Stroud, Oklahoma, hold an annual Pan-Indian event, as do the Tama Mesquakie, including older traditional observances; in 2000 there were still more than 700 speakers of the Sauk-Fox languages.

Kickapoo and Mascouten

The Kickapoo are an Algonquian-speaking people forming a dialectic group together with the Sauk and Fox, and more distantly with the Miami; their name derives from Kwigapaw, "he moves about here and there." Their original population was probably some 3,000, and they were first recorded by Father Allouez in about 1670, when they were living between the Fox and Wisconsin rivers. Le Sueur mentions them around the confluence of the Wisconsin River with the Mississippi. Their culture was essentially the same as that of the Sauk and Fox. They lived in bark lodges in the summer and oval reed lodges during the winter. They raised corn, beans, and squashes, but had a reputation for adapting to the Plains and Prairie environments when on hunting trips beyond the Mississippi – they learned to use horses in the early 18th century.

About 1765 they moved south into the country of the destroyed Illinois confederacy along the Illinois River near present-day Peoria, while another portion of the tribe established themselves along the Wabash River; these became known as the Prairie and Vermilion bands

Appanoosee, a Sauk warrior painted by George Cooke in Washington, DC, in 1837. Note the "gunstock" warclub fitted with a large metal trade blade, and decorated with brass nails. (Lithograph from McKenney & Hall)

A Sauk man from Indian Territory, possibly photographed during a delegation to Washington, DC, in c.1868. He is reputed to be a grandson of Black Hawk (1767–1838), who led resistance to the US in 1832. He wears a fur turban and a bear-claw necklace, and carries a horse quirt and a nail-studded warclub.

Kenakuk (c.1790–1857), the so-called "Kickapoo Prophet," was painted by George Catlin c.1830.

respectively. They played a major role in the history of the region, with Kickapoo warriors joining Tecumseh in his war against the US and the War of 1812. From 1809 they began a series of treaties with the United States, ceding all their lands in Illinois by 1819, after which they gradually settled in Missouri, Kansas, and even Texas. In 1832 a number of warriors rode with Black Hawk.

In 1852 a large party went to live in Mexico, followed by others in 1863. However, in 1873–74 a number of Kickapoo from Mexico were forcibly "encouraged" to return, and settled in Indian Territory (Oklahoma) close to the Sauk and Fox Reservation. The Mexican settlement became a focal point for disaffected and conservative Kickapoo. By 1885 only about 560 members of the tribe were reported in the US, of whom 235 were in Kansas and about 325 in Indian Territory. In addition, perhaps 200 lived in Mexico near the town of El Nacimiento in Coahilla, where they continued their traditional Prairie and Woodland culture adapted to the Mexican environment, and retained their language. During the 19th century the Mexican Kickapoo often joined Caddo, Cherokee and other Mexican bands on raids into Texas.

The Mexican and Oklahoma branches of the tribe have continued to vacillate in number throughout the 20th century, in pursuit of seasonal labour. In 1983 the Mexican members of the tribe obtained US citizenship, and land near Eagle Pass, Texas. In 2001 the Bureau of Indian Affairs reported 1,605 Kansas Kickapoo, 2,505 in Oklahoma, and 880 in Texas – the latter presumably all or most of the Mexican branch of the tribe. (Tribal membership requires one-quarter Kickapoo ancestry for qualification.) In 2000 there were about 500 reported Kickapoo speakers, probably mostly from the Mexican group.

The Mascouten are a little-known tribe, whose name comes from Mashkode or Muskuta ("prairie people") – a translation that has confused them with the Prairie band of the Potawatomi, who are unlikely to have any Mascouten ancestry. They seem to have lived in various places in present-day lower Michigan, but moved into Wisconsin via the southern end of Lake Michigan. They were visited in turn by Nicollet, Allouez and Marquette between 1634 and 1673, when they were in close association with the Sauk and Kickapoo. In about 1712 they were reportedly allies of the Kickapoo and Fox against the French and their Indian allies from the north. By the late 18th century they had been absorbed into the Sauk and Kickapoo.

Miami and Illinois (Illini)

The name Miami is believed to be derived from the Ojibwa word Omaumeg, "people on the peninsula," but this has been challenged. The Miami were an Algonquian people, living in the Green Bay area of Wisconsin when first known to European explorers, but by the end of the 17th century they were moving south toward the southern end of Lake Michigan, around Chicago and the St Joseph River. In 1703 there was a Miami village near Detroit. By 1711 they had reached the Wabash and Maumee and later the Great Miami River, the locations in Indiana and western Ohio with which they are historically associated. Their linguistic relations are closest to the Illinois tribes to their west, but culturally they were probably at one with the Sauk and Fox.

They suffered from Iroquois attacks until 1701, when they were represented at the Montreal peace conference that ended Iroquois aggression against the western tribes. The dominance of French traders was challenged by the establishment of the new Miami town of Pickawillany on the upper Great Miami River, which opened up trade with the British from Pennsylvania until 1752, when Pickawillany was destroyed by the French with Ottawa help under their mixed-blood leader Langlade (q.v.). Generally, however, the Miami supported French interests during the inter-colonial warfare of the 18th century. After the French defeat in 1760 they abandoned their eastern Ohio territory to the Shawnee and Wyandot.

After the American Revolution a complex coalition of Indian villages on the Maumee River became the center for Indian resistance to the organized efforts of the new US government and land speculators to purchase their territory. During the Indian war of 1789–95 the Miami under their chief Little Turtle defeated the Americans under Arthur St Clair (1791); however, following Gen Wayne's victory at Fallen Timbers (1794) they were forced to sign the Treaty of Greenville (1795). After the War of 1812 the Miami began to cede their lands to the US; although the combined population of the Miami and two subgroups, the Wea and Piankashaw, had probably been about 4,000 in the 17th century, the same grouping numbered only 1,400 by 1825. By 1845 only the Richardville, Godfrey, Lafontaine and Meshingomesia bands, mostly mixed-bloods, remained in Indiana; the remainder had moved to Kansas, and in 1867 they moved on again to Oklahoma. The Wea and Piankashaw joined the remnant Illinois under the combined name "Peoria," who also obtained a reservation in northeastern Oklahoma.

In 1903, just 191 Miami and 195 "Peoria" were reported in Oklahoma. In 2001 the Oklahoma Miami listed 2,677 enrolled, the Peoria 1,133, and several hundred others lived near Peru, Indiana, without federal recognition as Indians; all were of mixed descent. By 2000 there were no remaining speakers of either the Miami or Illinois languages.

The Illinois were an Algonquian confederacy of at least 12 subtribes, living principally along the Illinois River in that present-day state. The name Illinois apparently signifies "men" or "people." Little is known of their clan system or religion before the influence of French Jesuits. Father Allouez met a party of them in 1667 and 1670 within Wisconsin, but Marquette found others near the Des Moines River's confluence with the Mississippi, and the Kaskaskia division on the upper Illinois River. They were constantly harassed by the Sioux and Fox, and the Iroquois waged a long war against them due to their association with the French. During the French era in the western Great Lakes the numbers of Illinois dropped from around 6,000 to 2,000 through disease, alcohol abuse, and warfare – particularly with the Iroquois and Chickasaw. The murder of the famous Ottawa chief Pontiac in 1769 by a Kaskaskia Indian also provoked the vengeance of the Great Lakes tribes.

By 1800 only 150 were left; in 1832 the remainder sold their lands and moved to Kansas, and in 1867 on to Indian Territory. In Oklahoma they combined with the Wea and Piankashaw in the northeastern corner of the state, now Ottawa County, under the name "Peoria." These mixed-bloods of part French extraction

Paccane, a Miami warrior sketched c.1796 by Elizabeth Simcoe, wife of the lieutenant-governor of Upper Canada. He sports many silver ornaments, including a nose ring, and carries a trade tomahawk. (Archives of Ontario, Toronto)

A Shawnee man drawn in the Illinois country, c.1796. He has extended auricles (the rims of his ears) and lobes, and displays silver ear and nose jewelry and an armband. Under his blanket robe he wears a calico shirt and trade-cloth breechclout; his leggings are probably buckskin, with fringing and beaded garters. Note the length of his bow.

numbered 195 in 1905, on lands then allotted per capita; the same group's descendants were reported as numbering 1,133 in 2000.

Shawnee

The Shawnee, probably an ancient people of the Ohio region, are an Algonquian-speaking tribe whose closest linguistic relatives are the Sauk and Fox. Their name is derived from Shawunogi, "southerners," and although at least part of the tribe lived in the south they seem always to have maintained a firm friendship with northern groups. With an original population of perhaps 3,000, the Shawnee were separated into five divisions: the Chillicothe, Mekocke, Hathawekela, Piqua and Kispoko.

In the early historic period they moved to the Cumberland River valley in Kentucky and Tennessee, where French explorers first heard of them. In about 1674 some of the tribe had settled on the Savannah River, aiding the new British colony of South Carolina against local tribes. Early in the 18th century some of the southern Shawnee, of the Piqua and later the Hathawekela divisions, returned north to Pennsylvania, while others remained in the south with the Creek, with whom they have always had friendly relations. After about 1730, by permission of the Miami and Wyandot, many Shawnee collected on the north side of the Ohio River, along its tributary the Scioto.

The Shawnee had a long history as courageous warriors, and from the time of the French and Indian War until the War of 1812 some of them were in almost constant warfare against the British or the Americans. Eventually they were driven from the Scioto to the Great Miami and Auglaize rivers, and ultimately into Indiana; but in 1793 a number of Shawnee had moved to the then-Spanish territory west of the Mississippi in present-day Missouri, and later into Texas. In 1805 a Shawnee "Prophet," Tenskwatawa, began to preach a new doctrine which exhorted the Indians to return to the communal life of their ancestors. His followers were bonded into a confederacy under the leadership of the Prophet's brother Tecumseh. This prompted Governor William H. Harrison of Indiana Territory to move against their main village at Tippecanoe in September 1811 and, in Tecumseh's absence, the village was destroyed on November 7. Tecumseh led his remaining warriors north into British Canada; he would be killed there while fighting for the British, at the battle of the Thames River in 1813.

In 1825 the Missouri Shawnee, who had taken no part in that war, moved to Kansas, joined by others from Ohio, and in 1832 a band also mixed with Senecas from Ohio settled in Indian Territory. Shawnee from Texas, now known as the "Absentee" Shawnee, also settled in Indian Territory at various times between 1836 and 1859; after the Civil War, joined by Black Bob's band from Kansas, they finally settled in the southern part of the Potawatomi Reservation, Oklahoma. The Kansas Shawnees ceded their reservation to the US in 1854, and eventually agreed to move to Oklahoma to be incorporated into Cherokee Nation. Three separate groups in Oklahoma have remained on parts of their allotted lands to the present time, although predominantly of mixed blood, via the early adoption of white captives and intermarriage with French and British frontiersmen and with Cherokees. In 1909 their numbers were reported as 107 Eastern Shawnee, 481 Absentee Shawnee, and 800 Loyal Shawnee among the Cherokee.

After settling in the West the Shawnee showed prowess as herders of cattle and horses in trade along the Santa Fe trail. Unlike most tribes forced to live in Indian Territory, they managed to preserve some ceremonial and religious observances until recent times, particularly the Absentee Shawnee of the Little Axe Community in Oklahoma. Among the old ceremonies to survive were the Cornbread Dance, held annually in the spring and fall before planting and harvest, and the War Dance. One of the most important Absentee Shawnee rituals, this latter was traditionally an opportunity for warriors young and old to recount and relive their gallant deeds in battle. The War Dance also had a religious purpose, to give thanks at the height of the growing season to the Creator deity, "Our Grandmother" – whose female identification is unusual in Native American beliefs.

The census of 2000 gave 5,773 Shawnee; in 2001 the Bureau of Indian Affairs figures were 2,101 (Eastern Shawnee) and 2,926 (Absentee Shawnee), but the Loyal Shawnee in Cherokee Nation were not reported. A few descendants of the tribe are also reported from Ohio and Indiana, without federal recognition. There were then no more than 200 elderly speakers of the Shawnee language remaining.

WARS WITH THE WHITE MAN

Historical background

The beginning of recorded history for the upper Great Lakes Indians came in 1615, when the French explorer Champlain first saw Lake Huron. He was followed by expeditions to the Sault Ste Marie area and Lake Michigan by Brúle, Nicollet, Raymbault and Jogues, who in turn were followed by fur-traders in pursuit of beaver. The European impact on the native population was staggering: it changed migratory hunting and settlement patterns in order to satisfy the white man's desire for pelts, and the Indian demand for metal goods. A geographical rearrangement of tribes also followed the dispersal of the Huron by the Iroquois in 1649. Huron remnants joined the Ottawa who dominated the fur trade in the upper lakes, establishing new settlements at Chequamegon Bay, Michilimackinac and Detroit. These encouraged the establishment of Jesuit missions, and the fathers' annual "Jesuit Relations" give us the first descriptions of Indian life in the region. By the 1680s the Indians were also nominally under French military control.

By comparison with the Great Lakes area, the Ohio valley was relatively unknown to Europeans during the 17th century, since English westward expansion, blocked by the mountain barrier and by the Iroquois, was much slower. The Ohio country was inhabited by little-known semi-sedentary tribes, of whom only scant reports are known

Painted in old age in American clothing, the Shawnee chief Black Hoof (c.1740–1831) was a veteran of wars against the white man over 40 years, who had fought in "Braddock's Massacre" in 1755. He finally made peace with the Americans in 1795, and remained a voice for moderation thereafter. (Lithograph from McKenney & Hall)

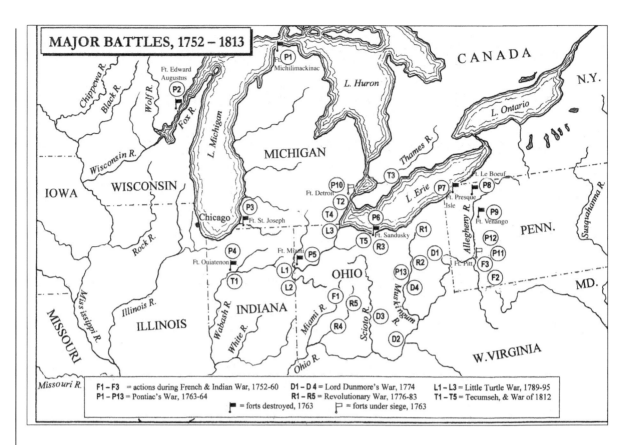

MAJOR BATTLES, 1752 – 1813

F1 – F3 = actions during French & Indian War, 1752-60   D1 – D 4 = Lord Dunmore's War, 1774   L1 – L3 = Little Turtle War, 1789-95
P1 – P13 = Pontiac's War, 1763-64   R1 – R5 = Revolutionary War, 1776-83   T1 – T5 = Tecumseh, & War of 1812
🚩 = forts destroyed, 1763   ⌐ = forts under siege, 1763

French & Indian War:
(F1) Pickawittany, 1752;
(F2) Washington's defeat, 1754;
(F3) Braddock's defeat, 1755
Pontiac's War: (P1) Ft
Michilmackinac; (P2) Ft Edward
Augustus; (P3) Ft St Joseph;
(P4) Ft Ouiatenon; (P5) Ft Miami;
(P6) Ft Sandusky; (P7) Ft
Presque-Ile; (P8) Ft Le Boeuf;
(P9) Ft Venango; (P10) Ft Detroit;
(P11) Ft Pitt; (P12) Bushy Run,
1763; (P13) Bouquet, 1764
Lord Dunmore's War: (D1) Yellow
Creek; (D2) Point Pleasant;
(D3) Salt Licks; (D4) Wakatomica
Revolutionary War: (R1) 1778;
(R2) Moravian, 1782;
(R3) Crawford, 1782;
(R4) Bowman, 1779;
(R5) Clark, 1780
Little Turtle War: (L1) Harmar,
1790; (L2) St Clair, 1791;
(L3) Fallen Timbers, 1794
Tecumseh, & War of 1812:
(T1) Tippecanoe, 1811;
(T2) Raisin R./ "Frenchtown,"
1813; (T3) Thames R./
"Moraviantown,"
1813; (T4) Ft Meigs, 1813;
(T5) Ft Stephenson, 1813.

before the Iroquois "Beaver Wars" of the 17th century violently dispersed them. Their resettlement of this region followed the general peace established by the French after 1701. The French made contact with the Illinois confederacy on the Mississippi by descending that river via the Great Lakes, not by a direct route via the Ohio from the east. The French connection quickly brought the Illinois under their influence and protection, but ultimately led to their near-destruction by the Iroquois, who at that period were enemies of the French. However, for 150 years the Indian peoples of the Ohio country fought with unparalleled bravery against colonialism, vacillating between France, Britain and the emerging United States in order to survive.

Gift-giving, and the French and Indian War, 1754–60

After the English supplanted the Dutch in New York in 1664, the Iroquois established relations with the new power in a treaty known as the Covenant Chain. In Indian metaphorical language the Iroquois had called their similar treaty with the Dutch the "iron chain"; the link to the English was an imagined "silver chain." The significance of this metaphorical chain was that it needed to be polished periodically with gifts, which were distinct from the ceremonial exchanges for wampum in diplomatic contexts.[2] The Indians gradually came to regard gifts as tokens of friendship, and as time passed they demanded more and more gifts from both the French and the English for renewing such friendships.

---

[2] Seashell wampum was traded as far inland as the Sioux. Since the Indians had no written language, woven belts of white and purple wampum shells in mnemonic designs, with superimposed painted colors signifying war, peace or friendship, were entrusted to important sachems (chiefs) to preserve records of treaties and agreements.

The Indians desired colorful cloth, blankets and ribbons, and iron knives, tomahawks, kettles, guns, silver gorgets, and medals; they also demanded food supplies, and alcoholic liquor. The actual distribution of gifts was accomplished in several ways. The French often allowed the Indians to come to designated forts or settlements, or to their missions for distribution by the clergy; the British often selected frontier rendezvous, such as Logstown in present-day western Pennsylvania. During the first half of the 18th century the Ohio country tribes often played off the French against the British and vice versa in order to obtain more and better presents. As well as securing military alliances, the relationships cemented by gift-giving helped traders obtain vast amounts of furs, and in time the Indians became economically dependent on the white man.

A striking painting by an unknown 18th-century artist of a warrior – possibly a Shawnee – scalping a British redcoat. He is shown with a feather headdress, and extensive face-paint in black, yellow, red and green; a red cloth breechclout, black buckskin or cloth leggings, and buckskin moccasins with ankle "collars." Note the incised silver armlets, the knife sheath hanging from his neck, the slung powder horn, and the metal tomahawk in his belt. The soldier is shown in an unlaced red coat with yellow facings.

Anglo-French competition in the giving of presents to the Ohio Indians carried on fairly peacefully between the Treaty of Aix-La-Chapelle in 1748, at the close of King George's War (1744–48), and 1751. However, the Ohio Company of Virginia and that colony's new Governor Dinwiddie had extensive schemes for purchasing native lands in the Ohio country with gifts of merchandize. This, combined with the parallel interest of the Pennsylvania colony in the Ohio country, prompted the French to employ aggressive measures in dealing with the Indians. When the Miami chief La Demoiselle (Old Briton, q.v.) switched his favor from the French to the Pennsylvania colonists, the French engaged with Indians who were not connected with the Covenant Chain, and a force of French Canadians and Indians swept down on the Miami trading village at Pickawillany in June 1752 and destroyed it – the unfortunate chief was boiled and eaten before the very eyes of his tribesmen.

This began a general French campaign to sweep all Pennsylvania traders out of the region, and the French military began to build a chain of forts down the west side of the Allegheny Mountains, with the object of bringing the whole Ohio valley under their control. The Ohio Company responded by trying to enlist the Cherokee to defend the disputed region, since the Iroquois were no longer strong enough to do so. The Virginians then sent the young Col George Washington to parley with the French; this, and a subsequent military attack, both failed, ending with Washington's surrender at Fort Necessity on July 4, 1754. The Ohio tribes were confused and divided, but gloried in their independence from Iroquois control.

The French and Indian War opened in this theater with the British Gen Edward Braddock's notorious defeat at the hands of the French and their Indian allies on the Monongahela River in July 1755, during an attempt to capture the French Ft Duquesne at the Forks of the Ohio (later Ft Pitt, and Pittsburgh.) Indians assisted the French in most parts of the Great Lakes region, including the tribes around Ft Detroit;

Indians delivering up white captives to Col Henri Bouquet at the Forks of the Muskingum River in November 1764 after the collapse of the so-called "Conspiracy of Pontiac." This Swiss-born officer was one of the British Army's most effective Indian-fighters from 1756 onward, and was the brigadier-general commanding the Southern District at the time of his early death in 1768. (Engraving after painting by Benjamin West, 1766)

the Huron, Ottawa, Ojibwa, and Potawatomi, and less frequently Delaware and Shawnee, attacked frontier settlements in Pennsylvania. Representatives of western tribes were operating as far east as Lake Champlain and Lake George in 1757 under the French mixed-blood Charles Langlade, and Sauk, Fox, Miami and Ojibwa were present at the fall of Quebec to the British in 1759. The war also saw Delaware and Shawnee settle in eastern Ohio after the British occupation of Ft Pitt in 1758; the Delaware moved to the Beaver and Tuscarawas rivers, and the Shawnee to the Muskingum (Wakatomica) and Scioto rivers.

As the French and Indian War neared its end, George Croghan, the right-hand man to Sir William Johnson (Britain's superintendent of Indian affairs, whose influence with the Iroquois and especially the Mohawk was important in the eastern Great Lakes theater) held a peace council at Ft Pitt with the Ohio Indians who had supported the French. Montreal was captured in 1760; that year the British assumed control of forts Detroit, Miami, and Ouiatenon on the Wabash, and in 1761 of forts Michilimackinac, Green Bay and St Joseph. The defeat of the French in North America was ratified by the Treaty of Paris in 1763, by which France forfeited to Britain everything east of the Mississippi except the enclave around New Orleans.

From Pontiac's rising to the Ft Stanwix treaty, 1763–68

London had given instructions to tighten American expenditure following the war, and the British, now in control of the western forts, abandoned the French practice of distributing presents – including giving powder and shot for hunting, and food in wintertime. This policy was applied by the British commander, Gen Amherst, against the expert advice of Sir William Johnson (Amherst's dislike and distrust of Indians even extended to an attempt to spread smallpox among them by the distribution of infected blankets). The Great Lakes tribes had enjoyed the camaraderie of the French fur traders, and the resulting mixed-bloods still traversed the area; the new policy led to serious hunger and consequent unrest among the tribes, and efforts to appease them by frontiersmen such as Croghan and Alexander McKee failed. Hostilities broke out in the spring of 1763 when a coalition of tribes was organized by an Ottawa chief, Pontiac (c.1712–69). In fact his overall involvement has been exaggerated, as it appears he may only have been present in person at the siege of Ft Detroit, and the defeat of the British detachment in the battle of Bloody Run.

The coalition of Ottawas, Ojibwas, Potawatomis, Shawnees, Mingoes and Wyandots (re-formed Hurons, now in the Ohio country) attacked and captured the lightly defended forts Sandusky, Miami and Ouiatenon. The sacking of Ft Michilimackinac is famous for the fact that the unsuspecting garrison opened the fort gates to watch a game of lacrosse being played by Indians; at a signal the warriors rushed into the

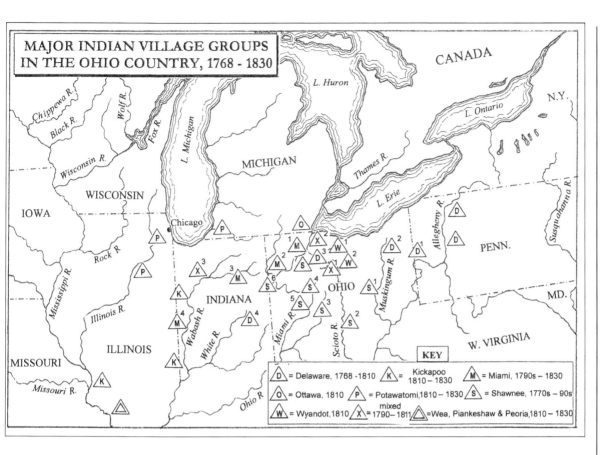

MAJOR INDIAN VILLAGE GROUPS IN THE OHIO COUNTRY, 1768 - 1830

KEY

△D = Delaware, 1768 -1810 △K = Kickapoo 1810 – 1830 △M = Miami, 1790s – 1830

△O = Ottawa, 1810 △P = Potawatomi,1810 – 1830 △S = Shawnee, 1770s – 90s

△W = Wyandot,1810 △X = mixed 1790– 1811 △△ =Wea, Piankeshaw & Peoria,1810 – 1830

fort, and few whites escaped with their lives. In all, eight forts were captured out of 12 in Indian Country, another was abandoned, and forts Pitt and Detroit were besieged; however, after six months the siege was lifted, and Pontiac himself later left for the Wabash and Illinois country.

The British retaliated; Col Bradstreet reinforced Detroit, and Col Bouquet turned an ambush into victory at Bushy Run while en route to relieve Ft Pitt in August 1763. The winter of 1763/64 was particularly harsh for the Indians, and the warriors melted away. Bradstreet offered peace terms in August 1764; that October, Bouquet took a strong force west to the Tuscarawas River, and by November he had forced the release of white prisoners being held by Indians at the Forks of the Muskingum River. The war gradually came to an end after the coalition was overawed by this display of British force, and Pontiac and his followers concluded a peace treaty with Sir William Johnson at Oswego, New York, in 1766.

In 1768 a major treaty was concluded at Ft Stanwix, New York, between the colonies and the Great Lakes Indian nations. A firm boundary was agreed; territories north of the Ohio River were to remain Indian country, but they were to relinquish much of Pennsylvania and lands south of the Ohio. The Shawnee would lose their hunting grounds in Kentucky forever, and were now a major belligerent faction in the multi-tribal villages lining the Ohio River's northern tributaries. George Croghan confirmed the agreement with the western tribes at Ft Pitt, and the old Covenant Chain was renewed with present-giving. Pontiac himself was murdered by a Kaskaskia Indian at Cahokia, Illinois, in 1769.

Key to numbered village symbols:
Delaware: (D1) Beaver R., 1768; (D2) Tuscarawas R., 1770s; (D3) Maumee R., 1790s; (D4) White R., 1810

Miami: (M1) Maumee R., 1790s; (M2) St Mary's R., 1790s; (M3) Wabash R., 1830; (M4) Lower Wabash R., 1810

Mixed tribes: (X1) Upper Sandusky R., 1790s; (X2) Maumee R., 1790s; (X3) Tippecanoe, 1811

Shawnee: (S1) Muskingum R., 1770s; (S2) Scioto R., 1770s; (S3) Little Miami R., 1780s; (S4) Mad R., 1780s; (S5) Great Miami R., 1780s; (S6) St Mary's R., 1780s; (S7) Maumee R., 1790s

Wyandot: (W1) Lower Sandusky R., 1810; (W2) Upper Sandusky R., 1810.

Tenskwatawa ("The Open Door"), known as "the Prophet." A brother of the Shawnee chief Tecumseh, he preached a religion of renewal at his village near present-day Greenville, OH, in 1805–07, and Tecumseh built a warrior coalition from the followers he attracted. He is shown wearing a red turban and hair headdress and crossed sashes, with a large silver gorget, and ear discs on long drops. (Lithograph from McKenny & Hall)

From Cornstalk's resistance to the Revolution, 1774–83

The 1768 treaty was mainly brokered by the Iroquois, and many Ohio Indians did not recognize the loss of their southern hunting grounds. Pennsylvania and Virginia now became the springboards for further westward expansions. Virginia, under its governor the Earl of Dunmore, seized control of the Ft Pitt region in 1773, and planned settlements west of the Alleghenies by issuing land warrants to veterans of the French and Indian War. In 1774 a gang of Virginians occupied the abandoned Ft Pitt, and massacred John Logan's Mingoes at Yellow Creek. Logan, at one-time a friend of the whites, now begged the Shawnee to help him take revenge; a few warriors attacked white settlers, which gave Lord Dunmore an excuse to crush the Indians. He launched a two-pronged attack, leading one force down the Ohio from Ft Pitt and sending another under Col Lewis down the Kanawha River toward the Ohio. Shawnees led by their chief Cornstalk made a furious attack upon Lewis' column at Point Pleasant at the confluence of the Kanawha and the Ohio. Although vastly outnumbered, they fought the Virginians to a standstill; but they lost many warriors, and finally had to return white captives and accept permanent white settlements in Kentucky.

Cornstalk's making peace with Dunmore led to a schism among the Shawnee during the American Revolution (1776–83). Cornstalk's Shawnees and White Eyes' Delawares saw no advantage in becoming entangled in a white man's war, but both leaders were killed by the Americans, and before the end of the war the neutral Shawnee and Delaware had rejoined their hostile kinsmen under the British flag along the Great Miami River, gradually withdrawing from the Scioto. The war-captain Blackfish continued to raid into Kentucky, and for a time in 1778 he held the famous Daniel Boone captive. Blackfish was killed in a raid on old Chillicothe in May 1779 by Kentuckians determined to repay the Shawnee for three years of war.

Through the efforts of the British agents McKee and the Girty brothers, an alliance of Ojibwas, Ottawas, Potawatomis and Wyandots also moved through the forests on expeditions against the frontiers of Kentucky and Virginia. Fierce Kentuckian counterattacks were led by Col Bowman in 1779 and Gen George Rogers Clark in 1780 on the Little Miami and Mad river villages, and in 1781 and 1782 by Brodhead and Williamson on villages on the upper reaches of the Muskingum and Tuscarawas rivers, some of which were Christianized settlements. In June 1782 the Pennsylvania militia under Col William Crawford were defeated by Wyandots and Delawares on the Upper Sandusky, but Clark again attacked villages on the Great Miami in retaliation for the British and Indian victory at Blue Licks. By the end of the Revolutionary War the Indians' grip on the Ohio country had undeniably been weakened.

From Harmar's failure to the Treaty of Greenville, 1789–95

After another Treaty of Paris ended the Revolutionary War in 1783, American agents informed the Indians that they must give up their claims to lands east of the Great Miami River and acknowledge the sovereignty of the new United States. After Col Benjamin Logan's attack

(continued on page 33)

JOLIET AND MARQUET MEET THE ILLINOIS, 1673
1: Illinois chief
2: Seated Illinois girl
3: Ottawa warrior, 1680

A

WARRIORS, 1720s–1780s
1: Winnebago warrior, 1780
2: Mesquakie (Fox) warrior, first half of 18th C
3: Ottawa warrior, 1755

WARRIORS, 1760s–1790s
1: Shawnee warrior, c.1774
2: Kaskaskia warrior, 1796
3: Great Lakes warrior, Pontiac War, 1763

C

CHIEFS, 1812–1832
1: Sauk chief Black Hawk, 1832
2: Miami chief, c.1830
3: Shawnee chief, War of 1812

RITUAL, 1890s
1: Ojibwa (Chippewa) singer
2: Midewiwin Society priest
3: Midewiwin lodge
4: Dream drum
5: Midewiwin instructor

E

SAUK, OJIBWA & MENOMINEE, 1830s–1870s

1: Sauk warrior, 1832
2: Shoppenegons, Michigan Ojibwa, c.1870
3: Sauk chief, 1860s
4: Menominee man, 1850s

F

WOMEN, c.1830–95

1: Sauk and Fox woman, 1880
2: Ojibwa woman with infant, 1830
3: Ojibwa woman, c.1895
4: Menominee woman, c.1830
5: Wigwams

THE 20th CENTURY
1: Ojibwa traditionalist, 1910
2: Ojibwa woman jingle-dress dancer;
Bad River Reservation, 1998
3: Mesquakie male dancer; Tama settlement, 1926
Background: Ojibwe Museum, Lac du Flambeau, Wisconsin

1

2

3

on villages along the Mad River in 1786, and continued American aggression, some chiefs agreed to sign the Treaty of Ft Harmar in 1789. However, unwilling to accept its terms, Miamis, Shawnees and others attacked settlers in southern Ohio, and in response the military launched a major campaign against the Indian villages now centered along the Wabash and Maumee rivers.

This was led in person by Gen Josiah Harmar of Pennsylvania, the commander of the then-tiny US Army, with some 300 regulars and 1,400 Pennsylvania and Kentucky militia. Harmar's June 1790 expedition from Cincinnati to present-day Ft Wayne, Indiana, was unsuccessful; although crops and several villages were burned, his force was twice ambushed, with more than 180 Americans killed. In 1791 the government sent a second expedition almost 2,000 strong against the villages along the Maumee, under the command of Arthur St Clair, governor of the Northwest Territory. They had reached the headwaters of the Wabash River by November 3, when they were routed by a large intertribal war party of Miamis, Potawatomis, Delawares and others under the leadership of Little Turtle. More than 630 militiamen and volunteers were killed, in what was probably the greatest single victory by Native Americans over a white military force.

Despite the end of the Revolutionary War the British still had troops in their old northwest territory; encouraged by promises of British help, tribal delegates who met American agents at Detroit in 1793 insisted that the whites leave the Ohio country. However, the US Army was being enlarged and reformed under command of the Pennsylvanian Gen Wayne, who belied his Revolutionary War nickname of "Mad Anthony" by his methodical patience in organization, drilling, and securing his advance with blockhouses. After an Indian attack on Ft Recovery was beaten off in 1794, that August Wayne led his 2,000-strong regular "Legion" and 1,000 Kentucky militia under Gen Charles Scott to a decisive victory at Fallen Timbers, near present-day Toledo, Ohio. He destroyed nine Indian towns, and the cornfields of the Delaware, Shawnee, Miami, Wyandot and Ottawa along the Maumee River. (Far from helping, the British closed the gates of their Ft Miami to the Indians. By the provisions of the Jay Treaty of 1794, the last British troops had left by 1796, although traders and settlers were allowed to remain.) Thirteen tribes were forced to agree to a new treaty at Greenville, Ohio, in 1795; other Indians, however, began to congregate beyond the Mississippi.

The Prophet, Tecumseh, and the War of 1812

During the winter of 1804–05, in a Shawnee village near the White River in Indiana, a man born to a family from an old village on the Mad River in Ohio had what may have been a drunken fit, and upon recovering his wits he told a strange story of death, heaven and resurrection. Over the following months Tenskwatawa, "The Open Door," experienced additional visions, and enlarged his doctrine of deliverance from the demoralized conditions in which the Ohio and Indiana tribes now found themselves.

He established a new village near Greenville, where some Shawnees and members of other tribes flocked to hear this new "Prophet." One of Tenskwatawa's brothers was Tecumseh, "Shooting Star," who had fought at Fallen Timbers and had refused to acknowledge the Treaty of Greenville. In 1807, when significant numbers of Indians with former British sympathies gathered to hear the Prophet preach, the Americans became apprehensive. Tecumseh and three other chiefs came to a meeting at Chillicothe, one of many at which protests were made against the continuing advance of white settlements, but these last appeals for coexistence were ignored. The Prophet was advised to leave the area by the now pro-American chief Black Hoof, and was invited to establish a new village called Prophetstown in Indiana.

Throughout 1808 tribesmen from Michigan, Illinois and Wisconsin came to hear the Prophet's revelations, and Tecumseh was quick to appreciate that a military confederacy could be built upon such religious enthusiasm. Nevertheless, many chiefs signed away millions of acres of land in Indiana and Illinois under the Treaty of Ft Wayne in September 1809. In 1810 and 1811 Tecumseh took an active role in demanding of Indiana's Governor William H. Harrison that these purchases be rescinded. In 1811 he traveled south to request that the Creek, long-time friends of the Shawnee, join him in alliance. However, in his absence Harrison marched along the Wabash with 1,000 men; arriving near Prophetstown on November 6, he provoked Tenskwatawa's followers to attack the following day, in contravention of Tecumseh's instructions. This battle of Tippecanoe was a complete defeat for the Indians.

Tecumseh then allied his warriors to the British in Canada during the War of 1812, and with some 600 men joined Gen Brock at the siege of Detroit. Despite their success, Perry's naval victory on Lake Erie cut the British supply lines and forced a withdrawal along the Thames River. Tecumseh informed Brock's successor Gen Proctor that he would withdraw no further, and unsuccessfully confronted an invading American force under Harrison at the battle of the Thames on October 5, 1813. Tecumseh was killed shortly after the battle; the warriors who had fought with him surrendered to Harrison at Detroit, and were later allowed to return to US territory. Tenskwatawa, the Prophet, reluctantly returned to American soil in 1825 and later moved to Kansas, where he died in 1836.

The Black Hawk War, 1832

This brief conflagration was the climax of a long sequence of events. The Sauk, Fox and Winnebago had been active confederates since the American campaign for the Ohio country and Indiana in the 1790s, and the Sauk helped the British in the War of 1812. After that war the Sauk became divided, between those under the eventual leadership of Keokuk, who were conciliatory toward the US, and those who were opposed to the treaties or chose to ignore them, led by Black Hawk (b.1767, so 65 years old in 1832). After the minor Red Bird "war" of 1827, the Sauk emerged as the principal core of resistance to American settlement in the western Great Lakes region. Concerted pan-tribal action against the Americans proved impossible due to serious quarrels with the Menominee and divisions among the Winnebago, leaving the Sauk faction led by Black Hawk, with some allied Fox, as the main protagonists against the Americans.

The war that broke out in spring 1832 was initially fought in northwestern Illinois, on the east side of the Mississippi and on the lower

Rock River. This was part of a large area that the Sauk and Fox had ceded to the United States by treaty in 1804. Thereafter, some Potawatomis along with a few Ojibwas and Ottawas had begun to occupy the region along the Mississippi between the mouths of the Rock and Wisconsin rivers. The 1804 treaty notwithstanding, in 1829 the US government made a treaty with these newcomers to grant them this part of the earlier cession. Most of the Sauk and Fox now lived on the western (Iowa) side of the Mississippi, except for Black Hawk's vacillating group, which were called by the Americans the "British band" in recognition of their former allegiance.

BLACK HAWK WAR, 1832

KEY:
- = Indian villages mentioned in text
- = minor actions
- = major actions
- = Black Hawk's route
- = forays by Black Hawk's warriors

At the time of the Black Hawk War, many Indian villages were spread along the shores of lakes Michigan and Winnebago, and the valleys of the Illinois, Rock and Wisconsin rivers and their numerous tributaries. Only those mentioned in the text, or near where actions were fought, are marked on this sketch map.

The Winnebago lived upstream on the Rock River pending their removal elsewhere, as they too had ceded their lands between the Rock and Wisconsin rivers in 1829. All the tribes had sold their lands reluctantly, in the face of superior white strength, and Black Hawk's defiance won him sympathizers and a number of active supporters among both the Potawatomi and Winnebago. Black Hawk's major Winnebago ally, the so-called Prophet (Wabokieshiek, or "White Cloud" – not to be confused with the earlier Shawnee Prophet), was half Sauk, and his village on the Rock River was located at present-day Prophetstown approximately on the boundary between the 1804 and 1829 land cessions.[3]

While most of the Sauk lived beyond the Mississippi, Black Hawk's band continued to return to their old haunts on the Illinois side of the river in order to plant and harvest corn. However, by spring 1831 white settlers had occupied the site of his home village, Saukenuk, and the newcomer Indians now lived on the Sauks' old lands. In response, a body of Sauk recrossed the Mississippi and commenced aggression against whites with the intention of breaking up the settlements along the frontier of Illinois. They reluctantly returned to the Iowa side of the river following pressure from MajGen Gaines and the governor of Illinois, abandoning their crops and facing hunger the next winter. In August 1831, the Sauk and Fox apparently attacked and killed a party of Menominee near Prairie du Chien. The following spring the Menominee planned revenge, and Gen Henry Atkinson alerted US troops at posts on

---

[3] So-called "prophets" preaching movements for religious and moral revitalization arose periodically among the Indians of the Old Northwest, and are often confused with the Shawnee prophet Tenskwatawa. A Delaware prophet attracted a following during the Pontiac War of 1763; Kenakuk (q.v.) had often been called the "Kickapoo Prophet," and at this time there was a comparable phenomenon amongst the Iroquois.

the upper Mississippi and at Ft Winnebago that a general Indian war might break out if the vengeful Menominees were not forestalled. White refugees exaggerated the numbers of Black Hawk's Sauk and Fox, and Atkinson was disinclined to move against such a large body of reported hostiles – even though his second-in-command Col Zachary Taylor had at least 1,800 mounted militia assembled by order of Gen Reynolds at Beardstown and other places along the Illinois River, and 400 regular infantry were at Dixon's Ferry on the Rock River by June.

In April 1832, Black Hawk had led his band of about 1,000 people, including some 500 mounted and armed warriors, across the Mississippi near Yellow Banks north of Tama. They reoccupied the old site of Saukenuk, and then proceeded up the Rock through their old territory, joining with some Winnebagos and Kickapoos at Wabekieshiek's village, and making forays further east. Although he insisted that he only wanted to plant corn, Black Hawk was intercepted and his emissaries were attacked by a party of 270 Illinois volunteers under Maj Isaiah Stillman, but in the consequent engagement Stillman's men "ran like deer" from a fight still known as Stillman's Run. Unwilling to face the large forces at Gen Atkinson's disposal, Black Hawk retired north and west to the swamps around Four Lakes, while still sending out war parties against isolated farms and settlements in southern Wisconsin.

Atkinson pursued the main body of Indians in the direction of Lake Koshkonong and Four Lakes, dividing his forces in an attempt to find them. Volunteers under Cols Dodge and Henry discovered the Indians' northwestward trail some 20 miles south of Ft Winnebago, and the subsequent battle of Wisconsin Heights left more than 60 Indians dead. At this point Atkinson was joined by 400 regular infantry under Col Taylor, and in all 1,300 men crossed the Wisconsin River in pursuit of the Indians on July 27 and 28, 1832. On the morning of August 2 they attacked, defeated and dispersed Black Hawk's main body on the banks of the Mississippi at Bad Axe Creek, killing more than 150 men, women and children. Few Indians were able to cross the Mississippi, since the way had been barred by the arrival, from Ft Crawford at Prairie du Chien, of a steamboat armed with a field gun. (Of those who did manage to cross, Wabasha's Sioux are said to have killed about 50, mostly women and children.)

Black Hawk, Wabokieshiek and other leaders escaped from the battlefield and headed north for the Winnebago village of Winneshiek on the La Crosse River. On August 27, after they were found in the vicinity of Tomah by the northern Winnebago, Black Hawk and the remainder of his band were delivered to the Indian agent at Prairie du Chien, Joseph Street – the northern Winnebago had been much less sympathetic to Black Hawk's cause than their southern kinsmen. This campaign was remarkable in retrospect for the later fame of some of the Americans who had taken part. Both Zachary Taylor and Winfield Scott saw service, though the latter arrived too late to see action. Abraham Lincoln was a lieutenant in Taylor's command, as was the future Confederate president, Jefferson Davis; the future Civil War general Albert Johnston also served, as did Daniel Boone's son.

After confinement at Jefferson Barracks, in the spring of 1833 Black Hawk, his son Neapope and Wabokieshiek were taken by steamboat and overland to Fortress Monroe, Virginia, and subsequently released. Black

Photographed in Washington, DC, in 1858, Peg-a-no-ke-shiek ("Hole-in-the-Day") the younger was an Ojibwa chief who succeeded his father of the same name as leader of the Crow Wing band in Minnesota. During an internal dispute in 1868 he was murdered by Indians from Leech Lake.

Hawk met President Andrew Jackson, and received much public attention in various cities during his return to Iowa, where he died on the Des Moines River in October 1838.

SOME INDIAN LEADERS

(Note: for the Shawnee Prophet **Tenskwatawa**, and the Sauk chief **Black Hawk**, see above.)

Black Hoof (*c.*1740–1831) A Shawnee chief who was present as a young warrior at Braddock's defeat on the Monongahela in July 1755. He continued to fight first the British, and later the Americans, until the Treaty of Greenville in 1795. Thereafter he was one of the chiefs who maintained the peace; they made concerted efforts to accept government help to pursue farming and erect permanent houses, and accepted overtures from various Christian groups (see also page 19).

Curly Head (or **Hair**) An Ojibwa (Chippewa) chief originally from Lake Superior, who moved to the Crow Wing area of Minnesota in c.1800. His warriors acted as a bulwark against the Sioux, and were friendly with white traders; he met Lt Zebulon Pike's expedition in 1805. Curly Head died while returning from a conference at Prairie du Chien in 1825.

Flat Mouth (*c.*1774–1860) A chief of the Pillager Ojibwa around Leech Lake, Minnesota. As a young warrior he took part in expeditions against the Cree, Assiniboine, and tribes on the upper Missouri, and his band suffered at the hands of the Sioux. He was succeeded by his son of the same name, who took part in a delegation to Washington, DC, in 1899.

Hole-in-the-Day A Mississippi Ojibwa who succeeded Curly Head as war chief in the vicinity of Crow Wing, Minnesota. He aided Americans during the War of 1812, and carried on a relentless war against the Eastern (Santee) Sioux until the US government forced acceptance of a line of demarcation between the tribes. He died in 1848 and was succeeded by his son of the same name, who was murdered at Crow Wing in 1868 (see opposite).

Kenakuk (*c.*1790–1857) A Kickapoo divine who founded a religious movement of mixed Christian and native beliefs among the Vermilion band Kickapoo and Potawatomi in the early 19th century; a church with about 100 adherents is still active on the Kickapoo Reservation near Horton, Kansas. The famous artist George Catlin painted Kenakuk in about 1830 near Leavenworth, Kansas (see page 16).

Keokuk (1767–1848) Sauk chief and contemporary of Black Hawk; leader of the pro-American faction of the combined Sauk and Fox after ceding all their lands east of the Mississippi. Made chief by the Americans, he obtained government agreement to Sauk and Fox claims to lands in Iowa; however, after the tribes were moved to Kansas they divided, the Sauk going to Indian Territory and the Fox (Mesquakie) back to Iowa. His son Moses Keokuk succeeded him, and continued to urge acceptance of the white lifestyle.

Charles Langlade (*c.*1729–1800) The son of a French fur-trader and an Ottawa woman, he led the French and Indian raid on the British-Miami settlement of Pickawillany

Keokuk (1767–1848), with his son Musewont or Moses. Keokuk, who led his people west of the Mississippi, was recognized by the Americans as chief of the combined Sauk and Fox from about 1830, while Black Hawk's followers remained unreconciled to the loss of their lands east of the river. This image is from a painting probably made by Charles Bird King in 1837. Keokuk is shown with a red (porcupine?) hair headdress; a red robe trimmed blue; a pale fur cape; a bear-claw necklace, and a peace medal; buckskin leggings with beaded blue, white and red strips; and red garters with ribbon bunches, large beads, and yellow-on-red beaded lappets. His son wears a pink shirt and a peace medal, and a blanket round his waist over plainer leggings; under magnification, his moccasins show an early representation of Prairie-style floral beadwork. (Lithograph from McKenney & Hall)

BELIEFS AND RITUALS

Among the tribes of the Great Lakes the Indians recognized supernatural spirits (Manitos) in all physical phenomena, animals, trees, rocks, or cosmic forces. Some dwelt in the sky, some on earth, underground, or underwater; some were helpful and others malevolent, such as ghosts, underwater monsters and cannibal ice giants (Windigos), and spirits were placated through prayers. Over all was a paramount deity, Kitchi-Manito, although this concept may be the result of Christian influence. Of major importance were the Sun, Moon, the Four Winds, the Four Directions, Thunder, and Lightning. Two great Manitos, the Thunderbird and the Underwater Panther, are dominant in Great Lakes mythology. The Thunderbirds were a class of spirits associated both with war, and with rain to nurture crops. The horned Underwater Panthers were greatly feared, but were also associated with healing powers. These two Manitos were often depicted as highly conventionalized images on woven bags and incised and beaded objects.

Of personal concern was a guardian spirit, acquired through vision quest, which would be called upon for help. Bear ceremonialism recognized the power of the animal, and those killed for food were ritually respected. Semi-divine culture heroes could take on human or animal forms to help mankind in a variety of ways, and were credited for bringing success in hunting or agriculture. Many of the southern tribes (e.g. the Winnebago) had an extensive range of sacred bundles, which were invested with supernatural powers that were maintained by reverent ritual, song and other complex observances, and were invoked to rid the world of evil spirits and giants. These bundles usually consisted of a skin bag containing mementos, significant pebbles, relics of animals and birds, carved fetishes, and so forth.

The religious life of the **Huron** was more elaborate than that of their Algonquian-speaking neighbors. They believed the world rested on the back of a great turtle, and that the supernatural Creator was a benevolent spirit who lived in the sky. His grandmother, however, seems to have been an evil spirit, and between them were numerous spirit forces with power for good or evil – similar to the Manitos of the Algonquian tribes. The Huron believed that after death their soul separated from the body and went to villages in the sky, or followed the Milky Way. In order to ensure reaching their respective soul-villages a major ceremony had to be held every 8, 10 or 12 years. This Feast of the Dead was a national ceremony, at which the dead from various villages who had initially been buried in shallow graves were exhumed, re-dressed or placed in beaver-skin bags, and after lengthy ceremonies were reburied in mass graves along with weapons, tools, food, utensils and robes for their journey to the sky-villages.

The religion of the **Ottawa and Potawatomi** organized a set of beliefs and ritual practices involving the concept of a Great Spirit, with deities of the Sun, Fire, and Water, and like all Indians they recognized spirit power in animals and natural objects. Personal guardian spirits were acquired through fasting and dreaming. After death, the human soul followed a trail over the Milky Way to the west, where there was a heaven. Later, both Ottawa and Potawatomi had the Midewiwin or Grand Medicine Society (q.v.), which functioned to heal the sick and prolong life. Cults were composed of members who had common dreams or visions. Ritual objects were contained in clan and Medicine Society bundles and bags, which were opened and used in ceremonials and feasts, when the eating of dogs was especially common. The dead were either buried, cremated, or placed on scaffolds. The **Winnebago** also had a version of the Midewiwin; their major ceremonies were the Winter Feast, to increase tribal war and hunting powers, and the Buffalo Dance, to call the buffalo.

War rituals

Various ceremonies were held before a war party went out, to enlist the power of guardian spirits to aid warriors and ensure success in battle. Warriors struck a post or tree with a warclub, and recounted the enemies killed in battle; others would dance, performing a variety of threatening attitudes of tracking, fighting, and scalping foes. Among the sacred objects invoked were the

A Winnebago war dance, Wisconsin Territory, c.1826. The figure at right has a tall, tiered feather headdress, a white shirt, and a natural-color blanket wrapped round his waist. Of the others, three warriors have all-red face paint, one half-red, and one red-over-black. The two at left foreground have a blue and a red trade-cloth breechclout with white stripes. The fifth from right has buckskin leggings with large, shaped lappets down the outside; the third from right has blue trade-cloth leggings with a yellow (beaded?) stripe, a bandolier and waist belt of blue edged with red, and moccasins with heel-feathers and red ankle-collars; and both these men have feather back-bustles. All carry ball-headed or gunstock-shaped warclubs, or metal pipe-tomahawks. (Detail from painting by Peter Rindisbacher; West Point Museum Art Collection, US Military Academy, West Point, NY)

war bundles, created under spiritual direction and opened during ritual offerings to supernatural beings associated with warfare. (In recent times the War Dance became the Chief's Dance, and has undergone a complete shift in purpose. The Woodland tribes have also adopted the Plains Grass Dance as a secular "war dance" for public events and modern powwows.)

The Midewiwin Society

The most important Woodland ceremonial complex, which survived until the 20th century (and in remote areas may still), was the Midewiwin or Grand Medicine Society, to promote individual and community success in hunting, good heath, wellbeing and long life. The geographical center of the religion was northern Minnesota; it is usually associated with the Ojibwa, and Ojibwa-derived terminology is used here, but it was also present among most of the Great Lakes tribes with only minor variations in rituals. The Midewiwln is said to have gained prominence around Chequamegon Bay and La Pointe, Madeline Island, Wisconsin, where a large body of Ojibwa had moved from the northern shore of Lake Superior during the early fur-trade era in the second half of the 17th century.

Rituals were usually held annually or semi-annually, and lasted from two to five days depending upon the number of initiates or candidates. Candidates were selected for membership by application, instruction, and formal invitation. The ceremony was presided over by an instructor or sponsor and a number of recognized priests, each of whom had assistants. At the beginning of the ritual the candidate, instructor and officiating priests were obliged to visit a sweat lodge, to appeal for a fine day and make offerings to the Great Spirit. They entered the Midewigan (large wigwam) where the spirit of Kitchi-Mainto resided, after circuiting the enclosure four times outside and inside. The candidate was led to the western end of the enclosure, where he knelt. The priest (Midas) held a medicine pouch containing the Megis (a shell), which he thrust vigorously toward the candidate's heart four times, as if to shoot him. This action in effect "shot" the vital spiritual power into the soul of the initiate, a baptismal act which aroused strong emotions. The priest then reapplied his medicine bags, and the candidate recovered, coughing out the Megis shell believed to have been shot into his body. This ceremonial "death and rebirth" initiated him as a member of the society; he then distributed trade-goods gifts as a form of membership fee.

There were at least four and sometimes eight major ascending degrees of membership in the Society, each representing the animal-spirit volunteers who transmitted the religion from the Creator to receptive individuals on Earth. The medicine pouches used in the first degree were often of otterskin or those of similar small animals, followed by hawk, owl, and bear, and, if applicable, eagle, wolverine, lynx, and finally snake. Each ascending degree of membership required fees of increasing value for the officiating priests, sponsor and assistants, while the new member was presented with a Mide pouch representing the degree to which he had been admitted. (See also Plate E.)

in 1752. At the head of a mixed band of warriors, he was present at the defeat of Gen Edward Braddock's command on the Monongahela River near Ft Pitt (then Ft Duquesne) in 1755; at Lake George in 1757; and at Quebec in 1759. After the American Revolution he settled at Green Bay, Wisconsin, and is considered one of the founders of the state (previously part of Michigan).

Old Briton or **La Demoiselle** A prominent chief of the Piankashaw division of the Miami, who emerged as the most outspoken critic of the French trading system in the 1740s. Enmeshed in the fur trade, the Ohio country tribes now needed the products of European technology to provide for their families, and Old Briton favored a switch to the less expensive and more plentiful British goods. Under the influence of the British trader George Croghan, in 1747 he led all the Miamis who would follow him to a new village, Pickawillany, on the Great Miami River in western Ohio. He refused French advances to return to their alliance, and as a consequence a large war party of Ottawas and Ojibwas led by Langlade (q.v.) destroyed the village and killed Old Briton. The French-allied Indians then boiled his body and ate it, as a perceived method of absorbing the power of an enemy.

Old Decora, or **Old Grey-Headed Decora** or **Kenoka Decora** (*c.*1747–1836) A mixed-blood

Ojibwa snowshoe dance, painted by George Catlin in 1835–37. This ritual gave thanks to the Great Spirit for the Indians' ability to continue hunting in winter thanks to their snowshoes.

The Potawatomi chief Wabaunsee (1760–1845), leader of the Prairie band; his name has had various translations, among them "The White Sky." After signing the Chicago Treaty following the Black Hawk War, he moved from the Fox tributary of the Illinois River across the Mississippi to lands near Council Bluffs, Iowa. Here he is shown with a black and white feather headdress with a fur band and red and green ribbons; a dark blue US military-style coat with gold epaulets; a peace medal, and what seems to be a gold braid neck ribbon. A serpentine line of red paint is shown running from above his left eye to below his right ear. (Lithograph from McKenney & Hall)

Winnebago chief whose warriors were staunch supporters of Tecumseh and his brother the Prophet; his Indian name was Schachipkaka ("War Eagle"). A Winnebago contingent fought with the British during the War of 1812 along the Sandusky River and at the battle of the Thames.

Orontory, or **Nicholas** (*c.*1695–1750) The Indian name of this pro-British Wyandot chief was "War Pole." The leader of a general conspiracy against the French in 1748, he plotted to attack Detroit, but his plans were thwarted when French officers learned of them. His actions split the Wyandot around Detroit, and his followers established new villages on the Lower Sandusky River.

Oshkosh (*c.*1795–1858) A Menominee chief, sometimes known as "The Brave." He and his warriors served with the British at Mackinac, Ft Meigs and Ft Sandusky during the War of 1812, and with the Americans during the Black Hawk War in 1832. He signed treaties with the US in 1836 and 1848. In 1842 his band of 105 families was located on the upper Wisconsin River, settling on the future Menominee Reservation in 1852; he died six years later on the Wolf River, Wisconsin.

Red Bird (*c.*1788–1828) A Winnebago chief living near Prairie du Chien, Wisconsin, and leader of a minor outbreak in 1827. Two of his people were arrested for killing a family of maple-sugar makers, upon which Red Bird killed two traders at Prairie du Chien. At Bad Axe Creek his band of about 37 men attacked a riverboat; they killed four of the crew, but lost at least seven warriors. He subsequently surrendered to the white authorities at Prairie du Chien, and died there on February 16, 1828; others of his band were later pardoned by President John Quincy Adams.

Sagaunash or **Billy Caldwell** (*c.*1780–1841) The son of William Caldwell by a Mohawk girl during his Revolutionary War service in Butler's Rangers. He served the British cause until about 1820, when he moved to the Chicago area and was appointed a nominal Potawatomi chief by his employers, the traders and mixed-bloods who were dealing with that tribe. He died near Council Bluffs, Iowa, in 1841. (The name "Caldwell" has also been used by a formerly landless mixed Potawatomi band originally from Point Pelée, Ontario, who did not move to the Walpole Island Reserve but whose descendants have lived in the greater Detroit area. However, any connection with Billy is almost certainly false.)

Tarhe or **"The Crane"** A Wyandot chief who fought under Cornstalk against the Virginians at the battle at Point Pleasant in 1774, and under Little Turtle at Fallen Timbers in 1794. However, after signing the Treaty of Greenville in 1795 he remained on friendly terms with the Americans. He helped Harrison negotiate the return of British-allied Indians from Upper Canada to the US at the close of the War of 1812.

Wabaunsee (*c.*1760–1845) A Potawatomi chief of their Prairie band, born near Greenville, Ohio. When known to whites his main villages were on the Illinois and Fox rivers in northern Illinois. After making a warrior reputation fighting the Osage, he was present at the so-called "massacre" by Potawatomis near Ft Dearborn (Chicago) in 1812, thereby giving Governor Harrison a reason to attack Indian villages in Indiana the same year. During and after the War of 1812 he signed various treaties with the US, including the second Treaty of Greenville (1814), the Wabash Treaty (1826), and the Chicago Treaty (1833), after which he moved beyond the Mississippi to near Council Buffs, Iowa. He died after an accident in Washington, DC.

THE GREAT LAKES NATIONS SINCE
c.1850

As noted above in the passages on specific tribes, the reservations in the northern Great Lakes area were created during and following the land cessions of the 19th century, when the Indians were forced to accept the dictates of the US government under huge pressure from white settlers. Their much-reduced land base forced the Indians to abandon their old ways of life as full-time hunters, gatherers and trappers, and the resources of the reservations were often controlled by corrupt government agents. As the Indians attempted to adjust to Euro-American culture they became divided between social groups such as Christians and pagans, mixed-bloods and full-bloods, progressives and conservatives. The Dawes Act of 1887 extinguished some communal titles, and divided tribal lands between individual Indian "allotments" and "surplus" lands open to white settlement, thus decreasing the land base still further. Gradually, attempts at non-Indian economic systems were adopted – farming, logging, commercial fishing, and off-reservation labouring work. Schools both on and off reservations effectively divided the generations, as younger Indians became detached from traditional lifestyles and values.

During the first half of the 20th century many Indians lived in poverty and poor health, but World War II saw many leave the reservations for military service and war work. The second half of the century was a period of increasing Indian control of reservation politics, economic programs, health and education – formerly the preserve of the Bureau of Indian Affairs, the government bureaucracy that still had overall control. Sometimes chronic disputes associated with tribal membership arose, as the gradual improvement in economic conditions during the later 20th century encouraged many individuals to seek tribal membership despite having less than the quarter-Indian ancestry usually required to qualify.

Most of the southern Great Lakes tribes were removed from their eastern forest and prairie locations to Indian Territory (now Oklahoma), often after brief stays in Kansas, obtaining reservations in the northeastern and central parts of the Territory. Pressure for the opening of Indian Territory to whites followed the Dawes Act, and persisted for many years. However, under the provisions of the Oklahoma Indian Welfare Act of 1936 many tribes were able to reorganize, with new constitutions and bylaws. Since then these Indian peoples have gained a measure of self-determination, with some farming, stock-raising, and employment in the oil and other industries. Over the years there has been much intermarriage, both with white Americans and among the 50 or so tribal groups represented in the state.

At the beginning of the 21st century only approximately 40 percent of an increasing Indian enrolled population lived permanently on the reservations, with large concentrations in major cities. A majority are of mixed blood, and tribal languages are now restricted to a few elderly people, if any.

O-ge-mah-o-cha-wub ("Mountain Chief"), an Ojibwa brave from Leech Lake, MN, photographed in the 1860s. He wears a white man's shirt, vest, and jacket, a trade blanket at his waist, an eagle feather in his turban, and a peace medal; he holds a pipe. (Photo J.E. Whitney, St Paul, MN)

Studio portrait, c.1900, of Be-mos-a-ge-shiek, an Ojibwa brave. He is resplendent in beaded yoke, sash, leggings and moccasins, with fringed arm- and wrist-bands. Note that he carries a "gunstock" club, and a catlinite pipe head without a stem.

Main-ans ("Little Wolf"), an elderly Minnesota Ojibwa photographed in Washington, DC, in 1908. Little Wolf was one of Frances Densmore's informants about the Midewiwin religion. He wears two eagle feathers in his fur cap, and a cloth shirt with appliqué beaded panels in a floral design. (Photo De Lancey Gill)

Ironically, in recent years the reservations' immunity from some provisions of the general US legal code have also seen the development of huge casinos and hotels, attracting many white tourists. These have brought enormous wealth, which has allowed the purchasing of land, and the establishment of tribally run museums and traditionally based courses of Indian lore for their children.

SELECT BIBLIOGRAPHY

Clifton, James A., *The Prairie People: Continuity and Change in Potawatomi Indian Culture* (Iowa City; University of Iowa Press, 1998)

Edmunds, David R., *The Shawnee Prophet* (Lincoln, NE, & London; University of Nebraska Press, 1982)

Herring, Joseph B., *Kenekuk, the Kickapoo Prophet* (Lawrence, KS; University Press of Kansas, 1988)

Hoffman, W.J., *Midewewin or Grand Medicine Society of the Ojibwa* (Washington, DC; 7th Annual Report of the Bureau of American Ethnology, 1891)

Howard, James H., *Shawnee: The Ceremonialism of a Native Indian Tribe* (Athens, OH, & London; Ohio University Press, 1981)

McKenney, Thomas L., & James Hall, ed. F.W. Hodge, *The Indian Tribes of North America* (Edinburgh; John Grant, 3 vols, 1933–34)

Quimby, George Irving, *Indian Life in the Upper Great Lakes* (Chicago, IL, & London; University of Chicago Press, 1960)

Sugden, John, *Tecumseh: A Life of America's Greatest Indian Leader* (London; Pimlico, 1999)

Tanner, Helen Hornbeck, ed., *Atlas of Great Lakes Indian History* (Norman, OK; University of Oklahoma Press, 1987)

Torrence, Gaylord, & Robert Hobbs, *Art of the Red Earth People: The Mesquakie of Iowa* (Seattle, WA, & London; University of Washington Press, 1989)

Vennum, Thomas Jr., *The Ojibwa Dance Drum: Its History and Construction* (Washington, DC; Smithsonian Institution Press, 1982)

White, Bruce, *We are at Home: Pictures of the Ojibwe People* (St Paul, MN; Minnesota Historical Press, 2007)

PLATE COMMENTARIES

Material culture and dress

Trees provided the basic materials for forest Indian life. Birchbark strips were used to cover the sapling frames of various forms of wigwam – oval, peaked, or pitched – augmented by woven reed mats, and held or sewn down with spruce roots. Spruce root was also used to edge bark containers. Birchbark was also used to cover canoes, over a frame of cedar ribs, floor sheathing, cross thwarts and gunwales. These were used by the more northern tribes, particularly the Ojibwa, Ottawa, and Canadian Indians, and as the fur trade increased they were developed into large canoes capable of transporting several men and loads

of furs over great distances. Indians were employed to make these fur-trade canoes, and were often part of the "brigades" that used them. In the southern regions, where bark was limited or of insufficient quality, dugout canoes were used, and lodges were covered completely with cattail mats.

Wood was used for the frames of snowshoes of various shapes and sizes, covered with a webbing of hide (*babiche*) and sometimes with painted symbolic designs to enlist the aid of animal spirits during winter hunting. Wood was also employed for toboggans, sleds, bows and arrows, war clubs of various forms (e.g. ball-headed or gunstock-shaped), for spoons and bowls often with carved and incised images, pestles and mortars, drums, flutes, lacrosse rackets and cradleboards. Wooden dolls were made as toys, as religious effigies to aid hunting, protect health, or as love charms.

The earliest credible images of Great Lakes Indians by European artists date from the late 17th century. Near-naked males are shown heavily tattooed and wearing only breechclouts and moccasins. A few men's skin shirts have survived from the 18th century, with tube-like fitted torsos and sleeves which may already show European influences. Most important to both sexes were hide robes and furs for winter use, and a number of robes have survived from the 18th century, enigmatically painted with mixtures of realistic and geometrical designs. Men's leggings of buckskin (and later cloth) were hitched to a waist belt; buckskin moccasins were basically the one-piece type common throughout eastern North America, with a central front seam, which was superseded by the style with a U-shaped vamp inserted over the instep. The porcupine-hair and turkey-beard roach headdress originated among the Woodland tribes to augment the warrior's scalplock, and ceremonial headdresses from the western tribes displayed buffalo horns and hair with quilled browbands. Decorated fur turbans, and spectacular necklaces of grizzly bear claws, were worn by men on ceremonial occasions.

It is probable that before European contact basic women's dress was a knee- or calf-length wrap-around deerskin skirt, usually with the edges meeting on the left side – a trait which continued with later trade-cloth skirts. In cold weather the upper body was wrapped with skin or fur robes or a poncho. Among the Ojibwa a slip-like dress hanging from the shoulder by straps and reaching to below the knees was known from the 18th century onwards. Decorative materials included dyed porcupine quills, occasionally bird quills, moosehair, sweetgrass, and other natural fibres. A number of objects have survived in museum collections from the 18th century, including painted robes from the western tribes; black-dyed buckskin pouches with quilled decoration of thunderbird and underwater panther symbols of the "upper and lower worlds"; painted buckskin tobacco bags with quilled fringing; and cradle decorations with thunderbird and lightning designs. Men wore finger-woven garters and sashes originally of native fibers and later of wool and yarn, with inter-spaced beads in diamond and zigzag designs, and bags of twined vegetable fiber or yarn were used by both men and women. Mats of woven cattail reeds dyed in various colors were used as floor or wall coverings in wigwams. Rawhide containers and boxes were produced by the western tribes.

Starting in the 17th century, a range of new materials became available from European fur-traders who brought blankets and other cloth in bulk, which became a substitute for buckskin in men's and women's clothing. The replacement of native fibers and sinew with European cotton thread also transformed Indian clothing during the next century. Women's blouses and skirts were decorated with beadwork, ribbonwork, and silver or German-silver brooches. New art forms such as cut-and-fold ribbonwork, originally from Maritime Canada, found their way to the western Great Lakes toward the late 18th century, and incising German silver for earrings and other jewelry also became popular. During the 19th century splint basketry and fine quilled barkwork, produced principally for the tourist trade (particularly by the Ottawa), also arrived from the east.

However, it was the arrival of Italian and Bohemian glass beads that transformed much Indian art, replacing shell, bone, seed and copper beads and gradually replacing quillwork on clothing. By the 19th century commercial thread-sewn beadwork had become the major decorative medium for ceremonial attire, using both weaving and appliqué methods. Floral designs predominated on late 19th century men's vests, leggings and breechclouts, and on dresses, blankets, leggings and blouses for women. Worn only on ceremonial and religious occasions, these spectacular garments reinforced ethnic and cultural identity during a period of oppression and loss of tribal cohesion.

Woodland material culture has made a strong contribution to Pan-Indian dress of the 20th century (see under Plate H), and one particular item of men's costume stands out – the beaded bandolier bag. Believed to be derived from both native and European functional prototypes, these were popular among most western Great Lakes Indians during the period 1850-1920, and particularly with the Ojibwa. These splendid mosaics of the art of beadwork, which survive in many museums and private collections, are silent memorials to the Great Lakes Indian peoples.

A: JOLIET AND MARQUETTE MEET THE ILLINOIS, 1673

A1: Illinois chief

In 1673 Louis Joliet and Father Jacques Marquette were the first known Europeans to locate the upper Mississippi from New France. They travelled with five companions in two canoes from the Strait of Mackinac via Green Bay, then across present-day Wisconsin, and in June 1673 they visited a village of mixed Mascoutens, Miamis and Kickapoos. The party reached the Mississippi near present-day Prairie du Chien, and Joliet and Marquette continued south until they reached an Illinois village. During their return they visited the Kaskaskia village on the Illinois River, and were back at

Ojibwa bark-covered peaked lodge, and canoe, in a detail from a painting made by Paul Kane near Lake Huron, c.1850.

Mesquakie wigwams or lodges covered with reed (bulrush or cattail), photographed in wintertime at their settlement at Tama, IA, c.1890. (Photo Hudson's Gallery)

Green Bay in September. The explorers were greeted by chiefs holding calumets (see under A3). Our image of this chief is inspired by four beautifully painted robes of the late 17th or early 18th century now in the Musée du Quai Branly, Paris, which are thought to be Illinois.

A2: Seated Illinois girl
The relatively small size of the surviving painted robes suggests that they were not used for winter warmth. Decorated with symbols of birds and protective designs, they could be displayed on any social or religious occasion.

A3: Ottawa warrior, 1680
A figure derived from the *Codex Canadensis, c.*1680 – a book of sketches (with a text thought to be by a defrocked Jesuit, Louis Nicolas), which have a spontaneity suggesting that they were drawn from life. The Algonquian tribes of the Great Lakes used shell wampum for adornment, suspending quantities from their extended earlobes and auricles; they also exchanged strings and belts with other tribes. This figure holds a calumet – a wand of feathers hanging from a decorative wood or reed shaft with or without a pipe bowl. Often in pairs, these were highly decorated, sometimes with beads and the necks of birds. Like wampum, the calumet pipe had mystic connotations particularly among the Algonquian and Siouan peoples, and tobacco was often smoked ceremonially to confirm solemn agreements – hence the concept of the "peace pipe." Calumet dances were performed for war or for peace, and were particularly important during treaty and friendship meetings between Indian tribes and with whites. The dance probably spread from the Mississippi and Ohio valleys eastward, from the Fox, Illinois and Miami, or through the Ojibwa and Ottawa to the Iroquois. From the same center, a westward shift spread to the pipestone quarry in SW Minnesota, where so-called "peace pipes" with red catlinite bowls were produced on neutral ground for warring tribes. Their ceremonial use was again widely diffused, over a range between Michilimackinac and the Plains.

B: WARRIORS, 1720s–1780s
B1: Winnebago warrior, 1780
He wears a buffalo (bison) headdress, to ceremonially call the buffalo before the spring hunt; at least two such headdresses survive, both with browbands of quillwork. In relatively recent historical times the buffalo ranged from the Wisconsin River as far east as Ohio, and the Siouan Winnebago seem to have shared some regalia with their

Menominee bark lodge, c.1900. It has a pitched roof and gable ends, and the bark panels are held in position by both inner and outer frames of saplings.

relatives on the Plains. Note the warrior's ball-headed wooden club, the fur garters often associated with warrior status, and wampum earrings and sash. The painted hand symbols on his chest were used by Mississippian tribes – perhaps from very ancient times – to indicate warriors touched in battle or slain in hand-to-hand combat. The Winnebago managed to maintain uninterrupted trade with the French during the 18th century, despite the wars between the French and the Winnebagos' friends the Fox.

B2: Mesquakie (Fox) warrior, first half of 18th century
In 1712 this tribe planned an attack on the French post at Detroit; though aborted, this provoked years of bitter conflict. This warrior armed with a bow and arrows is based upon a sketch drawn during the devastating wars that followed. Heavily tattooed, he wears a trade-cloth breechclout; from his neck hangs a quill-decorated knife sheath, and from his shoulder a similarly decorated black buckskin pouch strap. As a result of their heavy losses the Mesquakie subsequently joined the Sauk, the two tribes being collectively regarded thereafter as the "Sauk and Fox."

B3: Ottawa warrior, 1755
The Ottawa were famous traders, and formed connections with the French and their Huron allies through the early 17th-century fur trade. The defeat and dispersal of the Huron and Petun by the Iroquois in 1649 resulted in some combined Huron/Ottawa communities in various Great Lakes locations, and bands of both tribes subsequently settled in the Detroit and Sandusky River region, allying themselves with the French during the French and Indian War. This warrior's attire reflects a merged Great Lakes style. Cloth blankets with bands of ribbons were becoming available from white traders; note the trade-silver ear decorations and armbands, a shell gorget, and wampum-bead necklace and bracelets. He holds a metal trade pipe-tomahawk of European manufacture, a gift with symbolic significance that was often presented to Indian leaders. Metaphorically, to "take up the hatchet" meant to declare war, and to "bury the hatchet" universally meant to make peace.

C: WARRIORS, 1760s–1790s
C1: Shawnee warrior, c.1774
The Shawnee lost their Kentucky hunting grounds after the 1768 Ft Stanwix treaty, but their scattered groups gathered in the Ohio country and vigorously resisted white encroachments from Virginia. Based on a sketch from life, this warrior wears a woollen trade blanket, possibly English; black buckskin leggings with quillwork decoration; and moccasins with ankle collars, typical of the Woodland tribes. His silver ear decorations might be either traded, or produced by Indian smiths. Note the saber-shaped wooden war club.

C2: Kaskaskia warrior, 1796
This leading sub-tribe of the Illinois confederacy suffered continuous wars with the Wisconsin tribes and the Iroquois, and lost great numbers from European-introduced diseases. Few were left by 1800, but a sketch from life in c.1796 shows a warrior with roached hair, ostrich feathers, a black-and-white headband with silver ornaments, silver ear-spools and armbands, a quilled knifecase, and an iron tomahawk. The last of the Kaskaskia joined the "Peoria" – remnants of several Illinois and Miami groups – and ultimately found a home in Oklahoma.

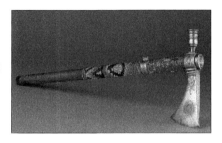

Metal pipe-tomahawk, of a type made in England for the Indian trade, c.1770. This finely engraved example, with a sun symbol on the blade, is of presentation quality. The haft is wrapped with porcupine quillwork added by the Indians. This piece was formerly in the Thaw Collection. (Photo John B. Taylor; Fenimore House Museum, Cooperstown, NY)

C3: Great Lakes warrior, Pontiac War, 1763
This warrior, from the coalition of Great Lakes tribes that rose against the British, wears a French military-style hat and coat. His green trade-cloth leggings are based on museum examples, showing the earliest appearance of ribbon appliqué work during the second half of the century – probably an influence from Indians further east and north. Note the quilled pouch, the belt, and the triangular porcupine-quilled knifecase at his neck.

D: CHIEFS, 1812–1832
D1: Sauk chief Black Hawk, 1832
This image of Black Hawk is partly based upon a painting, probably by George Bird King, made in 1837 during the chief's second visit to Washington, DC. His first visit followed his defeat in present-day Wisconsin in 1832, when the captured Black Hawk was taken on a tour to show him the power of the Americans, and was presented with a peace medal by President Jackson. He is depicted with the porcupine-hair roach, traditionally worn in battle to augment the scalplock.

D2: Miami chief, c.1830
A number of Miamis had left Indiana by 1827, and by 1845 only the Meshingomesia band remained in their old location. These were mostly mixed-bloods of part-French origin, or descended from captured colonists. One young girl taken by Delawares in 1778 near Wilkes Barre, PA, married a Miami and had four children; the man depicted here holds the silver cross that belonged to this woman, Frances Slocum (who died in 1847). On formal occasions Miami leaders of this period wore a mixture of Euro-American and Indian dress, including the use of traded ostrich feathers, silver gorgets, armbands and headbands, together with traditional items such as moccasins.

D3: Shawnee chief, War of 1812
After the collapse of his coalition in 1811, Tecumseh threw in his lot with the British during the War of 1812, until he was killed at the battle of the Thames River in 1813. Although no known authentic image of the Shawnee chief exists, this figure depicts probably contemporary objects. The shirt is based on a museum example now in Liverpool, UK; it is of dyed buckskin with silver and shell chest discs and quillwork attachments. He holds a ball-headed wooden warclub with a stone point – a deadly weapon, often incised with pictographic war accounts.

E: RITUAL, 1890s
19th–20th century rituals
Two main religious complexes, distinct from the much older surviving Midewiwin, appeared on reservations and in settlements during the late 19th century. The **Drum** or **Dream dance** complex originated on the Plains and was brought to Minnesota and Wisconsin during the 1870s; it is probably a variant of the Omaha or Grass Dance of the Plains, but with certain quasi-religious features. It derives from the story of a Dakota (Sioux) woman fleeing from an attack by US soldiers. After she had hidden in a lake without food for several days, a spirit took her to the sky, where she was instructed about a ritual to bring peace between all Indians and whites. The cult spread eastward from reservation to reservation through several tribes. The ceremony revolved around a number of sacred drums heavily decorated with beadwork (see Plate E4). The ceremony usually lasted four days; it was held either in homes or outdoors in a specially constructed lodge, with singing, dancing, ritual smoking, and lengthy prayers offered for good health and brotherhood. Followers of the religion must be of good moral character.

The **Peyote** religion is a Pan-Indian phenomenon that incorporates elements of traditional Native American religions and Christianity. Although it originated in Mexico, it became developed in Oklahoma toward the end of the 19th century; it has since spread to the Woodland tribes in Oklahoma and beyond, to such peoples as the Winnebago. There are two branches of the religion; central features of one of these are night-long rituals held in a Plains canvas tipi, to reflect the Plains origin of the ceremony and the interaction between the two cultural areas. Each participant holds a gourd rattle and feather fan, while a singer uses a Woodland-type water-drum. Eating peyote is considered a sacrament that allows contact with the Creator and the acquisition of powers, and the peyote leader is called a Roadman.

E1: Ojibwa (Chippewa) singer
Called "singers," these were usually also drummers – note the ceremonial water-drum. He is dressed in late 19th-century dark clothing heavily beaded with floral designs, including a vest of Euro-American style. During this period large bandolier bags became ethnic symbols and were produced in great numbers. Descended from smaller 18th-century powder and shot pouches, they had evolved by 1870 into large bags beaded in geometric designs. By 1880 many were decorated with floral appliqué (sewn forms) and had complex borders; finally they were fully beaded, without borders, and with only a slit for a pocket, which was sometimes omitted completely – they were now simply items of regalia, without practical function.

E2: Midewiwin Society priest
This Potawatomi priest (Midas) wears a variant type of bandolier bag, with bag and shoulder strap similarly beaded. He holds a medicine bag of otterskin, used for the ritual shooting and withdrawing of the shell (Megis) from the candidate for first-degree membership.

E3: Midewiwin lodge
Initiation ceremonies usually took place in a specially constructed lodge (Midewigan), sometimes open, or partly covered with bark or blankets on a frame of arched saplings.

E4: Dream drum
The ceremony involved prayers, songs and dancing, to promote friendship between tribes and even with whites,

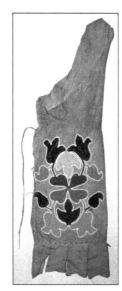

ABOVE: **Eastern Ojibwa bark box finely decorated with multi-colored porcupine quillwork, of a type that was being made for the souvenir market as early as c.1830–50. Formerly in the Thaw Collection. (Photo John B. Taylor; Fenimore House Museum, Cooperstown, NY)**

RIGHT: **Sauk or Fox (Mesquakie) buckskin pipe bag, c.1870, decorated with their distinctive beadwork – here in black, yellow, mauve, dark green, oxblood, dark blue and ochre. (Photo Ed Ogland)**

using a sacred drum often given by Indians from distant reservations. The decorated drum, with its associated canopy, was held above the ground on four curved supports. The example depicted was used at Lac Court Oreilles Reservation, Wisconsin. Note the drum beaters and rattles.

E5: Midewiwin instructor
A Society member who sponsored and instructed a candidate for membership before and during the initiation. This instructor wears a woven beaded bandolier.

F: SAUK, OJIBWA & MENOMINEE, 1830s–1870s

F1: Sauk warrior, 1832
This warrior of the Black Hawk War period holds a wooden "gunstock" warclub decorated with brass nails, and fitted with a metal blade. He also carries a horn quirt on his arm; many warriors of the southern Great Lakes tribes had become accomplished horsemen by the mid-18th century, and horses were used in the Black Hawk War. Note, again, the painted hand symbols – see under Plate B1.

F2: Shoppenegons, Michigan Ojibwa, c.1870
The Ojibwa and Ottawa of Michigan were among the first of the Great Lakes peoples to completely adopt Euro-American clothing. Only a few conservatives – such as this Ojibwa fishing guide, Shoppenegons, who worked on the Au Sable River until c.1890 – still used traditional attire on formal occasions. He wears a feather headdress, aprons, two-color cloth leggings, garters, bandolier bag, and silver gorgets. He holds a canoe paddle, confirming his status as a guide.

F3: Sauk chief, 1860s
This image is of a chief in the Sauk and Iowa delegation to Washington, DC, in 1867, the year that the Sauk movedto their final location in Indian Territory under their pro-American leader Moses Keokuk. He wears an otter-fur turban, a wrap-around blanket with ribbon appliqué, and rare so-called "front seam" buckskin leggings. The beadwork style on his leggings and moccasins probably developed during the time spent by the southern Great Lakes tribes in Kansas; this saw a merging of the several artistic traditions of the tribes forced to live there before finally moving to Indian Territory. He wears a bear-claw necklace, in reference to the belief that the animal possessed great spiritual power as well as physical strength, and he holds an eagle feather fan and a buckskin pipe bag.

F4: Menominee man, 1850s
He wears a turban and trade blanket, and holds a pipe with a carved-twist wooden stem. The bandolier bag is a transitional form, with a pouch panel of plaited wool yarn laced with white beads.

G: WOMEN, c.1830–95

G1: Sauk and Fox woman, 1880
Although the Sauk and Fox are regarded by the US government as one people, most of the Iowa branch are Fox (Mesquakie), noted for their finely decorated costumes. By the late 19th century these used mainly trade materials. The woman's hair is bound with beadwork, and her blouse is covered with small German-silver brooches. Her dark cloth skirt is decorated with cut-and-fold ribbonwork in abstract floral designs, and her blanket also shows ribbonwork. Buckskin moccasins with decorated collars complete her attire. Some designs used by the Sauk and Fox are thought to show the influence of Northern European settlers in the Midwest.

G2: Ojibwa woman with infant, 1830
The so-called "strap dress" – a knee-length garment with straps over the shoulders, and separate sleeves – may show an early European influence on an already existing buckskin form. The Great Lakes wooden cradleboard typically had a projecting, recurved head-bow, giving some protection. The Ojibwa had two methods of holding the baby to the cedar backboard: their northern bands used a lace-up cloth bag, as here, and the southern bands wrapped the child to the board with a wide cloth (see photo opposite). Some older cradleboards have protective carved designs.

G3: Ojibwa woman, c.1895
During the second half of the 19th century the Ojibwa used black velveteen cloth instead of the earlier black-dyed buckskin for their ceremonial attire, giving an excellent background for the colorful beaded embroidery for which Ojibwa women had an expert reputation. The bold floral beaded designs show European influence on an already existing curvilinear artistic tradition.

G4: Menominee woman, c.1830
The Menominee excelled in ribbonwork decoration. Silk ribbons were overlaid, shingled, cut and folded, then stitched to a cloth foundation – e.g. skirts and blankets – in curved or linear patterns. This craft had probably reached the Menominee from eastern Canada in the mid 18th century, perhaps via the French métis (mixed-bloods) around Green Bay, Wisconsin.

G5: Wigwams
Left to right: Sauk and Fox reed-covered lodge; Ojibwa peaked, birch-covered wigwam; dome-shaped lodge.

had moved west in the late 18th-early 19th century and had partly adopted Plains culture. The dark cloth dresses were decorated with rows of tin cones, which gave a jingling sound when dancing. The style soon spread to the Great Lakes Ojibwa, and during the second half of the 20th century it became a popular women's dancing costume, with contest categories for female dancers at ceremonials across the US and Canada. This dancer's dress is typical of the modern multi-colored materials and commercially-made cones.

H3: Mesquakie male dancer, Tama settlement, 1926

Fox (Mesquakie) warriors had been painted by George Catlin in the 1830s with regalia including porcupine-hair head roaches, and back-bustles made from the feathers of birds of prey attached to belts. These spread from the western Great Lakes and Prairie tribes to the High Plains peoples who were also forced to live in Kansas, Nebraska, and ultimately Indian Territory/Oklahoma. Probably while in Kansas, a number of tribes developed an abstract form of floral bead embroidery that during the 19th century became typical of Sauk, Fox, Potawatomi and Winnebago ceremonial regalia – particularly for male dancers' aprons, leggings and moccasins, and women's skirts and blankets. This figure represents the style worn by the Mesquakie at Tama, Iowa, in the period 1910–30.

(Background) Ojibwe Museum, Lac du Flambeau, Wisconsin

"Ojibwe" is the present preferred spelling. The George W. Brown, Jr, Ojibwe Museum and Cultural Center on this reservation offers visitors interactive exhibits and cultural programs.

H: THE 20th CENTURY

The process of acculturation has been very significant. Traditional homes and religious ceremonies were largely abandoned during the late 19th and early 20th centuries, except for special occasions and a few local exceptions. However, newer religions – the Peyote cult and Dream Dance (q.q.v.) – spread in Oklahoma from Mexico and the Plains. During the second half of the 20th century a merged intertribal phenomenon known as "Pan-Indianism" reinforced Indian identity in areas of social and political activity, and most visibly in regular powwows held on most reservations and in many communities. Male and female costumes, dances and parades reflect intertribal mixtures, but with a strong flavor of traditional Woodland traits and dress along with some quasi-religious features.

H1: Ojibwa traditionalist, 1910

Ojibwa men's distinctive traditional attire largely fell into disuse during the early 20th century as the old ceremonies were abandoned, and beaded costume and bandolier bags were often sold to museums, collectors and tourists. Since World War II, male regalia has reflected Pan-Indian influences from the Plains, but individuals continue to make and wear floral beaded vests, aprons and moccasins. This man wears black velveteen aprons and leggings decorated with floral beadwork; his buckskin moccasins are of typical front-seam construction, with a U-shaped beaded cloth vamp over the instep. His bandolier bag is the solidly beaded later type.

H2: Ojibwa woman jingle-dress dancer, Bad River Reservation, 1998

From c.1900 a new style of women's ceremonial dress appeared among the Plains Ojibwa of North Dakota and adjacent Canada. These people, descended from the Woodland Ojibwa,

Ojibwa bandolier bag, c.1900 – by now a purely ceremonial item of regalia, celebrating ethnic identity. This example is of appliqué multi-colored beadwork, with red tassels along the bottom. Such floral designs probably derived from both earlier native curvilinear decorative motifs and European folk art. The border designs are said to represent otter-tails. (Author's collection)

INDEX